WILLAN, Anne

How to cook absolutely
everything

how to cook absolutely everything

how to cook

absolutely everything

ANNE WILLAN

quadrille publishing

This edition published in 2005 by
Quadrille Publishing Limited,
Alhambra House,
27-31 Charing Cross Road,
London WC2H OLS

Based on material originally published in *Cooked to Perfection*

Editorial Director: Jane O'Shea
Creative Director: Helen Lewis
Editor & Project Manager: Lewis Esson
Design: Paul Welti
Design Production Service: Keith Holmes, Redbus
Production: Rebecca Short

Cataloguing in Publication Data: a
catalogue record for this book is
available from the British Library

ISBN 1 84400 203 9

Printed and bound in China

Contents

Introduction

This book began in the kitchen, as does much in our house. 'That looks done to me', I said one day as a student lifted a roast chicken out of the oven. And then I thought – how do I know? Cooking is a skill learned by experience, and nothing is more difficult than judging when a dish is cooked just right. All the senses are involved – smell, sight, touch, even hearing, with taste the last and most important of all. That roast chicken smelled heavenly; it sizzled; it looked brown and crispy, and when I wiggled a joint, it was loose. Provided the bird had been properly seasoned and basted I knew it must taste good, and it did!

From that brief beginning has developed what has proved to be an ambitious project. From the start I decided we must redefine traditional clichéed phrases such as 'until the fish flakes when tested with a fork' or 'until the cake springs back when lightly pressed with a fingertip'. We need to describe clearly and accurately in text and pictures how food looks, smells and feels when it is perfectly cooked. To illustrate this ideal state, often under- and overcooked shots are needed as well.

Then I realized it's no good explaining what is wrong without going on to put it right. So I do also often try to tell you what to do, suggesting cheerful garnishes, appropriate seasonings for bland food, and how to remedy technical problems like curdled mayonnaise or sticky pastry dough. I've also tried to help by giving as much advice on buying, storing, preparing and cooking the various foods discussed as space would permit.

Food and hygiene

The best advice is to use food promptly, keeping perishable items in a well-regulated refrigerator, at around 4°C/40°F. Store cooked and uncooked foods separately, wrapping them well. Keep track of how long your purchases have been stored in the refrigerator or freezer (bacterial activity doesn't stop in the freezer, it just slows down). If there is any question of possible spoilage, throw the food out.

Clean cutting boards thoroughly between uses. Exercise special caution with raw chicken and eggs, taking them from the refrigerator only just before you are ready to prepare and cook them. Those with limited or impaired immune systems, like the very young, the elderly, pregnant women and invalids, should not risk salmonella poisoning by eating lightly cooked poultry or lightly cooked (or raw) eggs.

Certain E coli bacteria are dangerous and have been found in the food chain, notably as a result of poorly handled beef. Be sure the surface of all beef you prepare is well cooked. Ready-cooked meats can be a hazard, as can minced meat products that have not been thoroughly cooked to the centre. Pork must always be thoroughly cooked.

The above cautions notwithstanding, many cooks still use raw eggs, (e.g. in mayonnaise) or enjoy dishes featuring lightly cooked eggs, 'pink' duck or hamburger. This book covers such techniques, but be aware that eating food prepared this way increases the risk of falling ill and can be life-threatening to the vulnerable.

ANNE WILLAN

Fish & shellfish

Fish and shellfish are surely the most difficult ingredients to cook just right. Their delicate textures and flavours can all too easily be ruined by overcooking, and a sensitive hand with the heat is important. Sometimes it's hard to tell exactly when they are done – swordfish and tuna, for instance, can be served rare, medium or well done, just like steak. However, we all recognize fish that has been overcooked to a soft mush, or shellfish that has been simmered so long that it becomes inedibly tough.

Fish species and fish names vary so much from country to country, even place to place, that it's incredibly easy to be confused. When shopping, I keep my eye open for the best catch on offer that day, rather than insisting on a particular type. Most fish recipes can easily be adapted to a range of similar fish, say plaice instead of sole, or snapper instead of sea bass. We are lucky to be offered such a range of wild fish, and it may not last much longer. I've nothing against farm-raised fish – on the contrary, inexpensive and reliable supplies of species such as salmon are a boon for everyone – but farmed fish tends to lack the individuality and intensity of flavour of a catch from the wild, particularly one which has been well handled and taken to market in timely fashion.

The first criterion when choosing fish is freshness, and your nose is the best guide. Very fresh fish and shellfish have a whiff of the sea, and taste that way too. Scales should be bright, eyes plump and clear, and shellfish should be heavy in your hand. Many shellfish, notably lobster, crab and bivalves like oysters should be alive just before cooking. Since it is important to know their origins and guard against pollution, a good supplier is your best friend.

Looking at flavourings for fish, I think at once of citrus (particularly lemon and lime), saffron, ginger, the anise taste of fennel and tarragon, plus star anise and the seed itself. Don't overlook the onion family, including leek, garlic and chives. Fish without wine, oil or butter and cream is unthinkable. Tomatoes, aubergines, peppers, celery, courgettes, potatoes and mushrooms all act as agreeable background vegetables, but there are many, many more. It is not so much the type but the amount of these accompaniments that is crucial. A whisper of Cognac or chilli with fish is divine, but a blanket can easily be a disaster.

THAI HOT-AND-SOUR PRAWN SOUP, PAGE 17

Fish fillets

Fish fillets should be rinsed and dried before cooking, then sprinkled with salt, white pepper (so the surface is not speckled with black) and any other seasoning called for in the recipe. When poaching and braising, be sure the cooking liquid is well flavoured. If frying or sautéing, the fat must be hot and the surface of the fish really dry, so it browns rapidly. Cooking time varies with the type of fish as well as the fillet's thickness. Plaice or flounder, say, can overcook in seconds, but meatier fish like monkfish and Dover sole are more resilient. Dry overcooked fillets can be moistened with a dab of melted butter. A sprinkling of crunchy chopped spring onion or celery will help soft, mushy fish, and a sprinkling of lemon juice, white wine, soy sauce or olive or other full-flavoured oil will lift bland fillets.

STAGES IN COOKING

▶ **PERFECT LIGHTLY COOKED** – surface firm and opaque or lightly browned, depending on cooking method; when tested with a knife, fish resists slightly, showing translucent inside layer. For most types of fish, this layer should be about 5 mm/¼ inch thick; oily fish like mackerel should always be well done.

◀ **PERFECT WELL-DONE** – surface of fillet very firm and opaque or browned, depending on cooking method; when tested with a knife, fish flakes fairly easily with no translucent layer inside; when lifted, it still holds firmly without splitting.

Fish steaks

Fish steaks offer all the versatility of fish fillets, though the bones and skin that often come with them make them less popular. Remember that it is the bones that hold steaks together and they also add considerable flavour to mild fish.

Easier to deal with are the boneless, skinless steaks cut from giant fish such as tuna, swordfish and shark. They can be thick or thin. as you prefer, and when carefully cooked they retain generous juices. Note that such fish may still have a rare centre if very lightly cooked. For most steaks, this translucent layer should be about 1 cm/³⁄₈ inch thick; oily fish like mackerel should always be well done.

I think the best cooking method for steaks is to grill or pan fry them with a minimum of fat. For garnish, look towards Mediterranean herbs, tomatoes, capers, olives and anchovies, or a more northern julienne of leek and carrot.

As with fillets, dry overcooked steaks can be moistened with butter or vinaigrette. The remedies for mushy or bland fish also work. More substantial steaks can also take more forceful flavour boosts like chilli oil or garlic.

STAGES IN COOKING

▶ **PERFECT LIGHTLY COOKED** – when tested with a knife, the centre is resistant, with translucent inside layer; surface opaque or lightly browned depending on cooking method.

◀ **PERFECT WELL-DONE** – when tested with a knife, flakes to show no translucent layer inside; surface is opaque or browned, depending on cooking method.

▶ **OVERCOOKED** – texture is soft or stringy, tending to fall apart; meat dry and shrivelled; edges of steak split and flesh shrinks from any central bone; if sautéed or pan-fried, surface may be scorched.

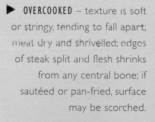

◀ **PERFECT LIGHTLY COOKED/PERFECT WELL-DONE** – when pressed, centre and edges of fish will be spongy/firm. Flesh will cling to any central bone when lightly cooked; bone will feel loose when well done.

Whole fish

Whatever the flavouring, a whole fish needs plenty of it to penetrate the flesh. If you like, season the fish – including the stomach cavity – thoroughly in advance and return it to the refrigerator for an hour or two before cooking so the flavours are absorbed. So the fish cooks more evenly, slash the thickest part of the fillets on the diagonal on each side and tuck in a herb sprig or a half-slice of lemon. The slash will shrink attractively to display the flesh. As a guide to cooking time, measure the fish at its thickest point, using an upright ruler. Allow 10 minutes' cooking time per 2.5 cm/1 inch. Bland fish and overcooked fish that's either dry or mushy can be helped in the same ways as for fillets (page 10) or try a tasty nut oil or a butter or velouté sauce. Serve disappointing whole fish with lots of distracting brightly coloured vegetables.

STAGES IN COOKING

▼ **UNDERCOOKED** – when tested with a knife or fork, flesh at thickest part of fish (here salmon trout) is resistant and shows a translucent layer clinging to the bone; on larger fish the eye is still translucent; if baked, barbecued, grilled or pan-fried, skin is still soft, not crispy.

▲ **PERFECT** – when a knife or fork is inserted at thickest part of the fish, flesh nearest the bone flakes easily and is no longer translucent; eye of fish is opaque; if baked, barbecued, grilled or pan-fried, fish is attractively browned, skin slightly crisp. Note: large fish will continue to cook from residual heat, so stop cooking when slightly underdone. However, light cooking (see Fish fillets and Fish steaks, pages 10-11) is not recommended as it makes a whole fish on the bone hard to carve.

▶ **PERFECT** – fish (here trout) flakes easily when tested near bone with a fork, and flesh is no longer translucent; eye is white; if baked, barbecued, grilled or pan-fried, skin is brown and crispy.

▼ OVERCOOKED – eye sunken; if baked, barbecued, grilled or pan-fried, skin is dry, often scorched, and flesh is dry and stringy, falling easily from the bone; if braised, poached or steamed, skin splits, gills gape and flesh starts to shrink from the bones.

SMALL WHOLE FISH

Leaving small fish on the bone, with the head, adds lots of flavour. If possible, the stomach should be emptied through the gills to avoid the cut edges curling open; if the stomach has been slit, skewer the edges together with a cocktail stick. For symmetry, serve all the fish with their heads to the left – this way not only do they look good, you'll find they are easier to dismember on the plate. Tests for cooking small fish are the same as for larger ones – they should just flake easily near the bone. I find the eye a particularly good indicator as it will turn white when the fish is just done. Note that small fish overcook in just a few minutes.

Whole lobster

Look for a lively lobster, heavy in its shell with plenty of meat. If boiling, allow 5 minutes for the first 500 g/1 pound and 3 minutes more for each extra 500 g/1 pound; if steaming, 8 minutes for the first 500 g/1 pound and 4 minutes more for each extra 500 g/1 pound. Thoroughly season the water for boiling, allowing 1 tablespoon salt per litre/1⅔ pints of water, and add white wine, vinegar, parsley and dill stalks, bay leaf, star anise and peppercorns; dried hot red pepper is an option. These, minus the salt, are good when steaming. For steaming and boiling, the lobster is kept whole, the claws often bound for ease of handling. For dry cooking, the lobster is usually halved lengthwise and the claws cracked, exposing the flesh to the heat of the oven, etc., making it easy to extract. If the cooked tail meat is tough, slice it across the grain and moisten with an olive, nut or chilli oil. Pep up bland hot lobster with a garlic, chilli and tomato sauce, or a garlic mayonnaise if cold.

STAGES IN COOKING

▼ **UNDERCOOKED** – shell tinged blue-black (for clawed lobster), or still pink, not red (for spiny lobster); tail only starting to curl under body; meat is chewy, clings to shell and looks translucent (for whole lobster, pull off a leg); greenish meat in chest section is soft, not set when edge of shell is lifted.

▲ **PERFECT** – shell bright red; tail curls under but remains pliable; inside, meat is tender, moist and white, just starting to pull away from shell (for whole lobster, pull off a leg and crack open to test); lift up shell of chest section – greenish meat inside should be set, not liquid; for halved lobster, meat is lightly browned, moist and tender; when tail meat is cut, centre is opaque, not translucent; flavour full-bodied.

Whole crab

Whole crab must be boiled with plenty of seasoning, allowing 1 tablespoon of salt per 1 litre/1¾ pints of water and adding vinegar, bay leaf, star anise, dried hot red pepper or cayenne. Disguise overcooked crab with a piquant dressing or sauce flavoured with chilli. If it is dry, moisten it with mayonnaise, yogurt-based dressing or vinaigrette. Bland or tasteless crab can be used for crab cakes or devilled crab.

STAGES IN COOKING

OVERCOOKED AND TOUGH – shell white and chalky; tail curled tightly under body and stiff; often body separates from tail; meat is fibrous, dry and shrunk from shell; often claws fall off; fresh flavour is lost.

UNDERCOOKED ► – shell still partly brown, pink or blue, depending on species; inside white meat is partly translucent and clinging to shell; brown meat is not set.

◄ PERFECT – shell bright or brownish red; inside flesh is starting to pull away from shell and brown meat is set; meat is succulent and cream-coloured, with sweet slightly spicy flavour.

Shrimp, prawns & crayfish

It's best to buy all of these raw in the shell (live for crayfish), so you control the cooking. When boiling, season the water with 1 tablespoon of salt per 1 litre/1¾ pints of water, adding bay leaf, star anise, peppercorns, mustard seed, dried chilli, thick slices of fresh ginger or lemon and 1 whole onion. Use these, minus the salt, for steaming, or you may like to try a spicy mix of dried chilli and coriander. Be sure to rinse and drain the shellfish before you use them. If peeled, dry on paper towels, season well with salt, pepper, soy sauce or cayenne, and leave them to absorb the flavours, 10-15 minutes. If they get overcooked and dry, serve with a savoury cheese sauce, tomato salsa or butter sauce. If bland, moisten with a shallot, garlic, thyme and lemon juice dressing. Sprinkle soft or chewy shellfish with nuts, like cashews or browned flaked almonds.

STAGES IN

COOKING

▼ **UNDERCOOKED** – shells may have some trace of blue or grey, depending on species; shells soft when pinched; meat is still slightly translucent and clings to shell.

▲ **PERFECT** – shells a deep pink with no trace of blue or grey, depending on species; shells firm when pinched; shells are slightly loose and can be peeled easily from meat; inside meat is white tinged with pink, plump and succulent; for peeled shellfish, meat is juicy, a pearly white, lightly or deeply tinged with pink depending on species; flavour is sweet and slightly spicy.

Thai hot-and-sour prawn soup

There are two schools of thought on this classic Thai soup. Traditional Thai cooks leave all the flavourings in the soup so the diner has to extract the edible parts. Westerners often strain out the flavourings before adding the prawns and mushrooms. Feel free to adjust the amounts of chilli and lime juice to your taste, remembering that balance between the hot and sour flavours is the key.

OVERCOOKED – shells dry, starting to lose colour and crack easily when pinched; tail very tightly curled; meat is shrunken, fibrous for large prawns, pasty for small ones; worst of all, fresh sea flavour is lost.

SERVES 4-6
500 g/1 pound medium raw prawns, in shells
small bunch of coriander
3 stalks of lemon grass
400 ml/13 fl oz coconut milk
125 g/4 oz straw or thinly sliced button mushrooms
2 tablespoons Thai fish sauce
juice of 1/2 lime, or to taste
salt

FOR THE FLAVOURED STOCK
1 tablespoon oil
2 garlic cloves, finely chopped
4 kaffir lime leaves, or pared zest of 2 limes
white pepper
2-4 fresh chilli peppers, cored, seeded and cut into thin strips

Peel and devein the prawns, reserving shells. Strip and chop the leaves from the coriander, reserving the stems. Cut the dry leafy tops from the lemon grass and peel away (and reserve) the outer layers to reach the moist tender cores. Crush the core with the flat side of a knife and thinly slice it.

Make the stock: heat the oil in a medium pan, add the prawn shells and sauté until pink, 2-3 minutes. Add the garlic and reserved outer lemon grass layers, and sauté, stirring, until fragrant, 1-2 minutes. Stir in 750 ml/1 1/4 pints water, the reserved coriander stems, lime leaves or zest, white pepper and half the chillies. Bring to the boil, cover and simmer until well flavoured, 20-25 minutes.

Strain the stock into another pan, stir in the coconut milk and bring to the boil. Season the prawns with salt and add to the stock with the mushrooms and sliced lemon grass. Simmer until the prawns and mushrooms are just done, 2-3 minutes. Stir in the fish sauce, remaining chillies, lime juice, and chopped coriander leaves. Taste and adjust hot and sour flavourings. Serve at once, while still very fragrant.

Shucked clams, mussels & oysters

Before shucking and cooking, clams, mussels and oysters must first be well scrubbed, discarding any open shells that do not close when tapped – they may be dead. If any shells are very dirty before shucking, it is wise also to clean the meat inside with a soak in sea or salt water for an hour or so to wash off sand and grit. Always remember that, on the half-shell, meat continues to cook in the heat of the shell. If it overcooks, you can dress meat on the half-shell with a drizzle of melted butter, oil or vinaigrette dressing, and sprinkle with chopped tomato, herbs, crisp bacon or, as contrast to a white sauce, a dab of caviar. For dry overcooked shucked shellfish, add a flavoured oil such as chilli or dark sesame, or vinaigrette dressing laced with shallot. If very overcooked, chop to serve in a lively salsa or in tomato sauce for topping pasta.

STAGES IN COOKING

▼ **PERFECT** – meat plump, juicy and just warmed through, with edges curled; flavour is sea-fresh and piquant; any coating or sauce lightly browned.

▲ **OVERCOOKED** – meat dry and shrivelled, aromatic flavour lost; a coating or sauce is often dried or separated.

Whole clams & mussels

Again, before cooking, both clams and mussels must be well scrubbed, discarding any open shells which do not close when tapped – these bivalves may be dead and should not be eaten. If the clam or mussel shells are dirty, it's a good idea to clean them by soaking in sea or salt water for an hour or two so the meat is purged of sand and grit. Mussels and clams are often salty, so do not add salt until cooking is finished, then taste them first. If the cooked results are still too salty, counteract this by adding bland ingredients like cream, tomato or potato. If, after cooking, the juices are still gritty, strain them through muslin; if the meat itself is gritty, nothing can be done. If clams and mussels get overcooked, they become almost inedibly tough, so the only answer is to use them in a pasta sauce, but first cut away and discard the neck of clams or the rubbery rings around mussels.

STAGES IN COOKING

▼ **UNDERCOOKED** – few shells open but most still shut. Check that the pan is tightly covered and that the heat is even, or stir contents of pan to distribute heat evenly, cover again and continue cooking, if necessary increasing heat.

▲ **PERFECT** shells open, with meat inside juicy and plump; smell is sea-fresh, flavour piquant. Note: if a few shells remain closed, discard them.

Scallops

Before cooking, season scallops with salt and pepper, having first drained them and dried them thoroughly on paper towels. Then give them a simple treatment, perhaps pan-frying them with fennel, or poaching them in cider and cream as in Normandy, or spearing them to grill on kebabs with cherry tomatoes, or baking them as a breadcrumb-topped gratin with onion, garlic and ham, as in Spain. Scallops take kindly to sweet spices such as cumin, coriander and saffron. Never, never allow them to overcook. If you should, or they don't have much flavour, try to disguise the fact by dressing them with a flavoured oil, melted butter or a vinaigrette, or serve with a butter or hollandaise sauce.

COOKING

STAGES IN

▼ **PERFECT LIGHTLY COOKED** – meat is plump and white or delicately browned, depending on cooking method; when pressed, meat offers no resistance (Thumb Test, first-finger stage, see right); flavour is sweet and aromatic.

▲ **PERFECT WELL-DONE** – meat is plump and white or lightly browned depending on cooking method; when pressed, meat resists (Thumb Test, third-finger stage, see right); flavour is sweet and aromatic.

▶ **PERFECT** – squid tender enough to cut with a thumbnail; juicy with no trace of toughness; flavour delicate, with a touch of salt.

THUMB TEST FOR FIRMNESS

A simple way to judge the cooking of a piece of fish, meat or poultry is to compare its resilience to that of your thumb muscle. As shown, the further the thumb has to reach, the more resilient the muscle becomes.

FIRST-FINGER STAGE

For lightly cooked fish and underdone/blue meat: touch your thumb to its opposing first finger and press the ball of your thumb with the tip of a finger of the other hand – the ball will offer no resistance.

SECOND-FINGER STAGE

For rare meat: touch your second finger to the thumb and press the ball of the thumb – it will feel spongy.

THIRD-FINGER STAGE

For well-done fish and medium-cooked meat, game or duck: touch your third finger to the thumb and press the ball of your thumb – the ball will feel resistant.

FOURTH-FINGER STAGE

For well-done meat or poultry: touch your fourth finger to the thumb and press ball of thumb – it will feel firm.

SQUID AND OCTOPUS

Squid and octopus used to be culinary jokes in non-Mediterranean countries. I well remember my Yorkshire-born father scoffing at a stew of squid in its ink, which I insisted on trying one year in Portugal.

No longer … We're all familiar with deep-fried squid, and may even have encountered char-grilled octopus or dishes such as pasta salad of squid with red onion, or Greek stuffed squid with rice, currants and lots of garlic.

They are not difficult to prepare; just remember that careful cooking is vital as both squid and octopus can turn so rubbery that you can't eat them.

They should either be very lightly cooked for a few moments, as when sautéed, deep-fried or poached, or simmered long and slowly in a Mediterranean-style stew with garlic, wine, olive oil, tomato and lots of herbs. At first they will toughen, then they gradually soften to be tender but still slightly chewy. A connoisseur's delight!

Deep-fried fish & shellfish

When deep-frying, all the action comes at the last minute, so efficient preparation is vital. Rinse the fish and pat dry. If using egg and breadcrumbs, coat the pieces ahead of time, then spread on a baking sheet and chill – this will dry the coating and make it all the crisper. However, coat with flour or batter at the last minute just before cooking. While the fat is heating to the correct temperature, assemble your equipment – frying basket, draining spoon or 'spider', and a tray lined with paper towel for draining. Even when using a thermostat, test the temperature of the fat with a drop of batter or a small piece of fish. It is essential that food is deep-fried at the right temperature or it will absorb too much of the fat and become greasy. Don't add too much food at one time, or the fat will take too long to come back to the right temperature. Drain the fried fish on paper towels and, if you need to keep it warm briefly while frying more, put it in a low oven with the door open.

STAGES IN COOKING

▶ **UNDERCOOKED** – batter or breadcrumb coating is pale, often soggy and falling from the fish or shellfish; inside, the seafood is firm, shellfish soft and partly translucent. You can drain undercooked food, reheat the fat to the right temperature and cook again briefly (in smaller batches if that was the problem).

◀ **PERFECT** – fish or shellfish is moist and opaque with no translucent centre; coating of batter or breadcrumbs is even and cooked to a crisp golden brown; flavour is juicy and full-bodied.

Seafood trio in beer batter

Here I suggest three favourite fish for deep-frying but many others work equally well. Buy what's freshest, if possible with a contrast of texture. Beer is a popular addition to batters as it cuts the richness of deep-fried food as well as making the batter light. I often serve deep-fried fish with an Oriental dipping sauce, but you can, of course, supply lemon wedges, mayonnaise or even tomato ketchup.

SERVES 4-6

250 g/½ pound salmon fillets, without skin

250 g/½ pound cod fillets, without skin

250 g/½ pound catfish or whiting fillets, without skin

45 g/1½ oz flour, seasoned with salt and pepper

oil for deep-frying

FOR THE BEER BATTER

150 g/5 oz flour

½ teaspoon salt

I egg, separated

300 ml/½ pint beer

I tablespoon vegetable oil

Make the batter: sift the flour and salt into a large bowl and make a well in the centre. Add the egg yolk with half the beer and whisk, gradually drawing in the flour to form a smooth paste. Stir in the remaining beer with the oil. Note: don't overmix or the batter will become elastic. Cover and leave to stand so the starch in the flour expands and lightens the batter, 15-30 minutes.

Heat oil for deep-frying to 190°C/375°F. Rinse the fish fillets and pat dry with paper towels. Cut each type of fish fillet into 4 equal pieces. Beat the egg white for the batter to stiff peaks. Fold the beaten white into the batter.

Coat the fish pieces with flour, patting to remove the excess. Dip a piece into the batter and lower it into the hot oil. Repeat with 3-4 more pieces and fry until done, 3-4 minutes depending on the thickness of the fish. Drain on paper towels and keep warm. Repeat with the remaining pieces of fish, frying them in 1 or 2 batches.

Arrange a piece of each fish on each of 4 warmed plates. Set a ramekin of dipping or other sauce beside the fish and serve at once.

Fish & shellfish stews

Almost all types of fish and shellfish can be added to a stew, the more the merrier, resulting in a wonderfully exotic range of flavours. Whatever the ingredients, guidelines for a fish stew are the same. Quick-cooking fish should be in large pieces, with slower-cooking types cut smaller. Add the different seafood according to cooking time, with those taking longest on the bottom. Be sure the cooking liquid is highly seasoned, and don't drown the fish – it should be barely covered.

▲ PERFECT – fish pieces firm and lightly cooked, with translucent line in centre, or well-done according to taste; shellfish plump, tender but still firm when pinched; sauce may be a concentrated broth or thick enough lightly to coat a spoon.

Stir-fried fish & shellfish

Asian cooks are expert at marinating seafood before stir-frying in piquant ingredients such as soy sauce, rice wine, lemon or lime juice, mirin, rice vinegar, fish sauce, or chopped garlic and ginger. They pay particular attention to chopping or slicing each ingredient to exactly the right size, and also to adding them in the right order at the right moment. Like deep-frying, stir-frying calls for quick reactions and careful timing. The process must be done at the right high temperature and don't overcrowd the pan or the food will steam or stew rather than stir-fry, losing its crispness. You can disguise soggy or overcooked stir-fried fish by stirring in crisp and colourful fresh ingredients like chopped celery, spring onion, radish, water chestnut or jícama. If your stir-fry is bland or otherwise disappointing, you can always season with more soy sauce, rice wine, lemon or lime juice, etc., or add in some fish sauce or Tabasco, or even some chopped lemon grass or spring onion.

STAGES IN COOKING

▶ **UNDERCOOKED** – fish or shellfish translucent on outside; other ingredients still almost raw so textures conflict and flavours have not started to blend and mellow.

◀ **PERFECT** – fish or shellfish is opaque outside and just firm; centre may be lightly cooked and translucent, or well-done as preferred; other ingredients are lightly cooked also, adding colour as well as crisp or smooth contrast of texture; flavours are lively.

▶ **PERFECT** – fish (clockwise from top: salmon, scallops and mackerel) moist; glossy and golden, not too dark; firm to the touch; flakes easily when forked; flavour full-bodied but not overpowering. (Stringy appearance denotes overcooking).

▶ **PERFECT** *right* – clear white or pink colour of fish (here salmon) slightly blanched by acid; good balance of acid and piquant, lively without overwhelming delicate flavour of raw fish. **OVERDONE** *left* – colour faded and patchy; fresh flavour of fish lost.

SMOKED FISH AND SHELLFISH

Smoking has long been used for preserving fish as the process prevents its fats from turning rancid. These days the emphasis is mainly on flavour. The texture of smoked fish and shellfish should be firm, but not tough. The flavour and aroma of the smoke should be evident and, depending on the process, it should colour the fish from light to dark amber.

In most cases, fish is salted or dipped in brine before being smoked in one of two ways. In cold-smoking, a true preserving technique, fish is exposed to cold (32°C/90°F) smoke, so it dries and pickles rather than cooks. Fish cold-smoked for 24 hours can be stored up to two weeks. This process is safest done commercially under strict controls. In hot-smoking, the fish is cooked by smoke at 38-88°C/100-190°F, which only partially preserves it. Hot-smoked fish should be eaten within a few days. Some hot-smokers have a chamber for liquids like water, beer or wine, which impart even more flavour to the fish as it smokes. Fish that has been hot-smoked too long looks shrivelled, with uneven colour and a sour smell.

MARINATED RAW FISH AND SHELLFISH

Recipes for marinated raw fish and shellfish fall into two main categories: very thin slices of fish that are sprinkled with flavourings, often called carpaccio after the Italian beef preparation; and Latin American seviche, with its spicy strips or chunks of fish or shellfish. In each case, the acid present in the marinade lightly cooks the fish. For carpaccio, the fish must be sliced wafer-thin so that the acid and other flavourings sprinkled on top penetrate quickly, for serving within a few minutes. A typical seviche is marinated with lime juice or vinegar and hot with chilli, but mild versions can be made with a simple vinaigrette. Marinating time can be lengthy, even a day or two, producing almost a pickle.

Fish for marinating must be super-fresh, and only a few firm, sweet-fleshed types are suitable. Salmon and scallops are prime favourites, though sea bass, plaice, white tuna, red snapper, sole and squid are very good as well.

Fish & shellfish pâtés & mousselines

These need well-flavoured shellfish or fish with a fine texture such as pike, whiting or scallops. Salmon is valued for its colour: avoid fish like mackerel and sardine as their high oil content can break down the pâté's texture. The raw seafood is finely puréed – a food processor is fine, though the traditional drum sieve gives a finer texture. Use only a stainless steel or nylon sieve to avoid discolouring the fish. Seasoning with salt helps stiffen and bind the mixture, and be sure to chill the seafood before beating in the cream. Before any cooking, test a ball of the mixture in gently simmering water to see if it falls apart; if it does, work in more egg white. At the same time, taste the cooked mixture and add more seasoning if needed. A water bath must be used to control the heat during cooking, as these delicate mixtures can easily separate.

STAGES IN COOKING

▼ **UNDERCOOKED** – mixture moist and disintegrating; when unmoulded and cut, sides sag and centre is soft; mixture offers no resistance when pressed (first-finger stage, see page 21); a skewer inserted in the centre for 30 seconds is scarcely warm to the touch when withdrawn; meat thermometer inserted in centre registers less than 70°C/160°F; flavour not yet developed.

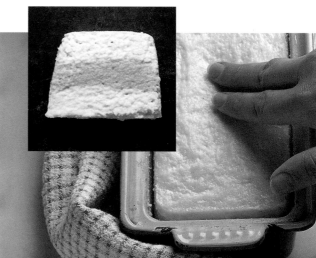

▲ **PERFECT** – texture of the pâté or mousseline is light and smooth, just holding firm; mixture is firm when pressed (fourth-finger stage, see page 21); a skewer inserted in the centre is hot to the touch when withdrawn after 30 seconds; meat thermometer inserted in centre registers 70°C/160°F; taste is subtle and fresh, with colour pale and clear.

▶ **PERFECT** – quenelles are lightly puffed, firm to the touch, and holding a clear shape. When cut, the texture is soft and smooth with fresh colour and definite flavour.

▼ **OVERCOOKED AND SEPARATED** – texture dry, rough and almost curdled; mixture discoloured and shrinks from sides, with juices expelled around edges; skewer inserted in centre for 30 seconds is very hot when withdrawn; thermometer inserted in centre registers 70°C/160°F or more; fresh flavour lost.

FISH QUENELLES

Quenelles, or dumplings, are closely related to mousseline, being basically the same mixture reinforced with a flour-based panade (often simply choux pastry). Most quenelles are of French origin, but a few ethnic recipes such as Jewish gefilte fish of pike bound with matzo meal also meet the definition. The dumpling mixture is firm enough to hold together if shaped with spoons and poached in stock or water. As it cooks, the quenelle puffs and lightens, floating to the top when done. When making quenelles it is important to poach a sample, both for consistency and taste. If the quenelle is heavy or tastes of flour, it is most likely underdone. If thoroughly cooked but still disappointing, I usually beat a whole egg or two into the mixture to lighten it. The mixture will probably also need more seasoning.

Poultry & game birds

How lucky we are! Can you imagine having to cook without a constant supply of inexpensive poultry that comes so conveniently in various forms – whole, in pieces, even boneless. Yet it was only in the 1950s that battery henhouses brought poultry within common reach. In my childhood, chicken was a treat, totally absent from school or weekday meals.

Now chicken has taken centre stage, its accommodating taste a strength as well as a weakness. Mild enough to blend with almost any other ingredient, chicken can be spiced up or left plain, mixed with vegetables, with meats like bacon and sausage, or even with shellfish such as prawns.

There's much debate on the merits of free-range chickens and I've yet to be convinced that any but the very best are worth the extra cost. What matters more is how the chicken was fed – some foodstuffs taint the meat. When it comes to duck, however, you'll find that the lean birds available through speciality outlets and Chinese markets are far superior to the average fatty supermarket variety. The same goes for whole turkey or goose, my personal choice. Here's where money is well spent on a cosseted free-range bird. The difference in flavour can be dramatic. Appropriate seasonings and accompaniments range widely for all four types of domestic bird.

I haven't even mentioned the most interesting poultry category of all, that of game birds. They are rapidly becoming domesticated in the sense that more and more farm-raised varieties are available, including ostrich, emu, pheasant, guinea fowl, wild duck, pigeon and quail, in descending order of size. Tenderness is almost guaranteed when they are cooked right, and flavour offers a mild adventure which I urge you to try.

Poultry, particularly chicken, adapts well to virtually every cooking method. The high heat of roasting and grilling assures crisp skin and uncomplicated flavour – the danger is dryness, for which you'll find all sorts of remedies in this chapter. With the lower, moist heat of sautéing, braising and poaching, flavours become more elusive; it's here that the French insistence on simmering sauces to reduce and concentrate them is so important.

ITALIAN STUFFED CHICKEN BREASTS, PAGE 41

Whole chicken
Baked, braised, pot-roasted, roasted

Dry the chicken inside and out with paper towel, then season the skin and cavity, or rub the skin with a dry marinade. If you can, return the bird to the refrigerator for 1-2 hours before cooking so the flavours permeate. You may also want to stuff it with a bundle of herbs, an onion or lemon. Always truss or tie it with string to keep its shape. So heat penetrates evenly, start the bird roasting on its back and, once it starts to brown, turn it from one leg to the other, then finally on its back. Constant basting is key. Let the bird stand in a warm place for at least 10 minutes before serving, so the juices are redistributed. You can moisten a dry overcooked bird or add flavour to a bland one with a piquant gravy, brown sauce or salsa.

STAGES IN COOKING

▼ **UNDERCOOKED** – cavity juices pink; skin pale and not crisp; when drumstick pulled, joint rigid; flesh resistant when pierced with a fork; thermometer between thigh and breast reads less than 83°C/180°F; carved breast meat tinged with pink and thigh joints very pink.

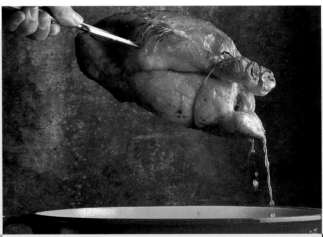

▲ **PERFECT WHOLE CHICKEN** – when lifted with fork, juices from cavity run clear; skin evenly golden and crisp; when drumstick pulled, joint feels slightly flexible; flesh plump and tender when pierced with fork, and just starting to shrink from end of leg; thermometer inserted between thigh and breast reads 83°C/180°F; when carved, meat moist with no trace of pink. Note: thermometer unreliable for chickens under 1.4 kg/3 pounds.

Whole chicken
Poached, steamed

Much of the advice opposite holds good here. Trussing is important, as the limbs will shrink from the carcass during cooking if left undone. For poaching, look for a large chicken, if possible an older bird (boiling fowl). It will take longer to cook, but have much more flavour. For maximum flavour when poaching or steaming, be sure the cooking liquid is laced with aromatics. To make a sauce, boil the liquid to reduce it well.

STAGES IN COOKING

▼ DRY AND OVERCOOKED – flesh stringy and shrinking from bones; skin may be scorched; leg collapses when end is pulled; if not trussed, cooking may be uneven.

▼ TOUGH AND UNDER-COOKED – when thickest part of thigh pierced, meat is resistant and juices run pink; meat wet and fatty, still pink-tinged, especially in gap between breast and leg; joint rigid when pulled; thermometer between thigh and breast reads less than 83°C/180°F.

▲ **PERFECT** – meat is tender and juices clear when thickest part of thigh pierced; chicken plump and meat just starting to shrink from end of leg; when pulled, joint feels slightly flexible; thermometer inserted between thigh and breast reads 83°C/180°F (unreliable for chickens under 1.4 kg/3 pounds.).

Whole turkey

The bigger the turkey, the lower the oven temperature should be, so that heat penetrates slowly and thoroughly without drying the surface. However, a temperature below 160°C/325°F is risky for large birds, as the heat can take too long to reach the centre and harmful bacteria may flourish. Stuffing also slows the cooking, so I prefer to leave the bird empty, and bake the stuffing separately in a large dish or individual dishes so it develops a crusty brown top. When the bird is done, let it stand in a warm place at least 10 minutes before carving so the juices are redistributed uniformly throughout the meat.

STAGES IN COOKING

▼ **UNDERCOOKED** – when drumstick is pulled, leg joint is rigid; skin is not yet crisp and meat looks flabby; juices run pink when thickest part of thigh is pierced with a fork; meat thermometer inserted between thigh and breast reads below 83°C/180°F.

▲ **PERFECT** – when drumstick is rotated towards breast, it feels slightly loose; skin is evenly golden brown and crisp; meat is plump and starting to shrink from end of leg; juices run clear when thickest part of thigh pierced; meat thermometer inserted between thigh and breast reads 83°C/180°F; when turkey is carved, meat is moist and full of flavour.

BONELESS ROLLED WHOLE CHICKEN AND TURKEY

Boneless whole chicken and turkey, tied in a neat cylinder for roasting, is almost as common as boneless poultry breast. It could hardly be easier to cook, behaving in the oven like a boneless pork or veal roast. Don't use too much liquid as the meat can be watery. Flavour is mild, so add plenty of seasonings and baste often during cooking. To dress up the roast further, before cooking remove the net or strings, open up the meat and spread it with a savoury stuffing or sprinkle it with flavourings such as chopped onion, garlic, shallot, fresh ginger or herbs, then re-roll and tie it.

Serve with lively garnishes such as a fruit conserve of baked figs, caramelized peaches or cherries, plus colourful accompaniments – braised red or green cabbage, green peas, orange lentils or pumpkin purée are just a start.

▲ **PERFECT BONELESS ROLLED CHICKEN** – meat thermometer in centre of meat reads 83°C/180°F; outside is golden and juices run clear when meat is pierced with two-pronged fork or skewer; a skewer inserted in centre of meat is hot to touch when withdrawn after 30 seconds.
Note: large pieces of rolled poultry will continue to cook inside from residual heat, so stop cooking when slightly underdone.

Poultry & game bird pieces

Chicken pieces offer a pleasant dilemma – do you choose a whole cut-up bird, thus giving diners a choice of colour and piece of meat, or opt for using only thighs, legs or breasts, so they cook at the same pace and are easier to handle? I'm never sure which way to go. In any case I try to season pieces before cooking, rubbing the skin with dried herbs such as herbes de Provence, or marinating them in wine or soy sauce. A full-scale wine marinade can also serve as a cooking medium. If your pieces get overcooked, take the meat from bones and pull into pieces for use in a pasta sauce or salad.

STAGES IN COOKING

▼ **TOUGH AND UNDERCOOKED** – juices run pink when pieces are pierced with fork, meat clings to fork; skin is pale; meat is flabby not firm.

▲ **PERFECT** – juices run clear when pieces are pierced with a two-pronged fork, pieces fall easily from fork; skin is evenly coloured; meat is firm, tender and moist; flavour is full-bodied.

Whole game birds

First make sure that your birds have been properly hung so that their flavour has fully developed. As they tend to be very lean, they will benefit from barding, wrapping in thinly sliced pork fat or bacon. Truss or tie the bird in shape and, during cooking, turn it from one leg to the other, finishing on its back. Most importantly, when roasting, baste often; if braising or pot-roasting, the birds need less attention.

STAGES IN COOKING

▶ **PERFECT LIGHTLY COOKED** – cavity juices pink; skin lightly browned; leg joint rigid; meat firm when thigh pierced; carved breast meat pink and juicy with mealy-to-gamy flavour depending on type and age. Legs will be tough and undercooked (often cooked on in stew).

▼ **DRY AND OVERCOOKED** – meat and skin shrink from bones; meat is stringy.

◀ **PERFECT WELL-DONE** – cavity juices clear; skin golden brown; meat shrinks from end of leg, which feels slightly flexible; carved breast meat well-done but still juicy and tender with meaty flavour; legs likely to be tough. Birds continue to cook from residual heat, so stop cooking when slightly underdone.

Whole duck & goose

Despite their richness, duck and goose can be dry if not carefully treated. My advice on seasoning and trussing of whole chickens (pages 30-31) also applies to duck and goose. Start cooking at high heat, turning it down once the duck or goose skin starts to brown. To allow the fat to be released, I prick the skin before cooking begins and then I baste often. You should set aside the excess fat to keep for frying the world's crispest potatoes.

Both birds make tasty gravy, but do be sure to drain off all fat before you deglaze the pan. If roasting, remember to let the bird stand in a warm place for at least 10 minutes before serving so the juices are redistributed uniformly throughout the meat.

If the finished results are very fatty, serve with a piquant orange, peppercorn sauce or gravy, and accompaniments such as pickled red cabbage or turnips.

STAGES IN COOKING

▼ **PERFECT LIGHTLY COOKED** – when carved, breast meat of duck is rosy pink and juicy; skin crisp and an even golden brown; when duck or goose is lifted, juices from cavity run pink; when leg pulled, joint is rigid, and meat is firm when thigh is pierced; a meat thermometer inserted between thigh and breast reads less than 83°C/180°F; full meaty flavour. Note: legs will be tough and undercooked and must be cooked further, usually by grilling.

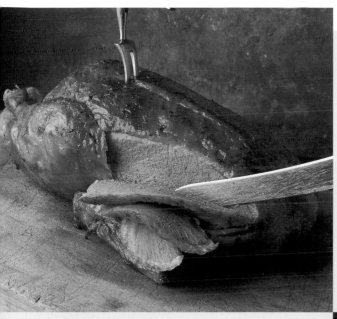

▼ **OVERCOOKED AND DRY** – when carved, breast meat is dry and stringy, shrinking from breastbone as well as legs; skin is dry, lacking brilliance, and may be scorched; leg falls from carcass when end is pulled.

▲ **PERFECT WELL-DONE** – when carved, breast meat is well-done but still juicy and tender; skin crisp and a deep golden brown; when duck or goose is lifted, juices from cavity run clear, not pink; meat shrinks from end of leg, which feels slightly flexible when pulled; a meat thermometer inserted between thigh and breast reads 83°C/180°F; generous meaty flavour. Note: legs will be well-done and tougher than breast.

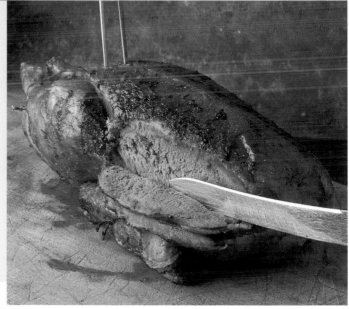

Split small birds

Marinating is a great help with little birds – try brushing them an hour or two before cooking with a light barbecue sauce, or perhaps with mustard, Worcestershire sauce or lemon juice and crushed bay leaf. To grill small birds, I often first 'spatchcock' them, splitting and skewering them flat so they cook evenly. Plump birds do well if the meaty parts are also slashed so heat penetrates more evenly. If your birds do get dry and overcooked., brush them with melted butter, oil or your basting sauce, and serve with a brown sauce or salsa. Oriental sauces like hoisin or plum are also good, then serve with relishes like mango chutney, or spicy pickled vegetable condiments such as chow-chow or piccalilli.

STAGES IN COOKING

▼ **UNDERCOOKED** – meat is pinkish and pink juice runs when thigh is cut with a knife; meat is flabby and skin may not be brown.

▲ **PERFECT** – meat of bird (here baby chicken) is evenly cooked throughout and white; juices run clear when thickest part of thigh is cut with a knife; skin is crisp and well browned with no scorched patches; meat is moist and full-flavoured.

Stir-fried poultry

Unlike most other poultry dishes, here vegetables and flavourings take equal place beside the meat. Lean meat, vivid flavourings and a good contrast of colour and texture are key. Breast without skin is my first choice of meat, though Oriental cooks are adept in cutting up a whole bird in neat chunks so the bones add taste. Poultry for a stir-fry is helped when first marinated briefly – five minutes makes a difference. See page 24 for more on stir-frying technique.

▼ **DRY AND OVERCOOKED** – meat stringy, skin scorched; little or no juice runs when thigh is cut.

▲ **PERFECT** – poultry is lightly coloured; texture still juicy; other ingredients add colour as well as crisp or smooth contrasts of texture; flavours are lively.

Boneless duck & game bird breasts

Think of duck and game bird breasts as a sophisticated steak and you cannot go far wrong. They offer all the advantages of rich, juicy meat, individual servings (sometimes enough for two) and robust flavour which invites an equally challenging accompaniment. Duck and game breasts also have the disadvantage of steak: they toughen dramatically when overdone and are best served pink or else baked or braised to be very well cooked indeed.

Domestic duck breast can be fatty so I always start by grilling or searing it in a hot pan, skin side down, until very brown and the fat is thoroughly rendered. Score the skin so fat dissolves during cooking. If you prefer, you can then discard the skin, though personally I regard it as the best part. By contrast, game bird breasts dry easily and should be browned with care and cooked in moist heat. If they get dry and overcooked., use a gravy or butter sauce with lively flavours such as cranberry, green peppercorn, blackcurrant or redcurrant. If the meat is tough, you can disguise this by slicing it very thinly across the grain.

STAGES IN COOKING

▼ **PERFECT LIGHTLY COOKED** – when tested with the point of a knife, meat inside is pink and juicy; skin is golden brown and crisp; feels spongy when pressed in centre with a fingertip (Thumb Test, second-finger stage, see page 21); flavour is full-bodied.

▲ **PERFECT WELL-DONE** – when tested with the point of a knife, meat is well-done but still juicy and tender; skin is crisp and deep brown, with fat (for duck) thoroughly drained; breast firm when pressed in centre with a fingertip (Thumb Test, fourth-finger stage, see page 21); meat is still full-flavoured.

Boneless chicken & turkey breasts

Such breasts do dry out easily, so it is thus a good idea to marinate them, however briefly, before cooking and to score them so moisture penetrates. They usually come stripped of skin and trimmed of fat. However, the underside has a sinew which toughens and shrivels during cooking. To remove, loosen the white, visible end with a knife. Grasp tightly with a cloth and strip it out with the finger and thumb of your other hand.

PERFECT – when pressed with your fingertip, meat feels spongy (Thumb Test, second-finger stage, see page 21); breast falls easily from a two-pronged fork and juices run clear; meat is moist, full-flavoured and tender.

Italian stuffed chicken breasts

Serve this summer dish, with chopped peeled tomato warmed in olive oil and lemon juice, with more chopped basil.

SERVES 4

4 skinless, boneless chicken breasts, sinews removed (see left)
small bunch of basil
2 thin slices of cooked ham
8 thin slices of Mozzarella cheese
salt and pepper

Preheat oven to 190°C/375°F/gas5. Strip the basil leaves from their stems and reserve 4 sprigs for decoration. Cut each ham slice in half, to about the same size as a Mozzarella slice. Set a piece of ham on top of a cheese slice. Lay 2-3 basil leaves on top and cover with another cheese slice, to make 4 packages.

Butter a medium baking dish. Turn breasts skin side down and remove and reserve the loose strip of fillet. Turn breasts skin side up. Cut a horizontal pocket, working the whole length of each breast and taking care not to cut all the way through.

Stuff each pocket with a ham package and then the reserved strip of meat, tucking it in to seal the gap. Set skin side up in the baking dish. Season, cover tightly with foil and bake until done, 30-35 minutes.

When the chicken breasts are done, slice at an angle and arrange each in a fan on individual warmed plates to show the stuffing. Top with a reserved basil sprig.

Meat & Game

Of all main-dish ingredients, I find meat is the most forgiving. A hint of dryness, a few minutes' overcooking, a drab appearance – all can be taken care of with little trouble, as I hope to show you in this chapter.

For a start, let's look at the general characteristics of the different meats. Beef is juicy and full-flavoured but is apt to be tough. Bold flavourings come to mind, such as mustard, paprika, chilli powder, horseradish, red wine and garlic. To complement lamb, the other domestic red meat, I tend to turn to the Mediterranean and capers, olives, rosemary, thyme and garlic, not forgetting the mint from my mother's English garden. Given how differently veal cooks from beef, you might never think it comes from the same animal. As a young meat, veal is rarely tough but it can easily be dry; plenty of liquid and no more than medium heat are advisable. Veal's flavour is best developed with lemon, nutmeg, mace, rosemary, parsley and white wine … and don't stint on the cream, butter or olive oil. Pork, the other white meat, is wonderfully rich and varied – think of all those chops, hams and sausages which are so good with honey, apples, brown sugar, sage and spices. Despite its richness, however, pork dries easily, just like veal.

As for game, toughness is the great danger, especially with wild meat. When making sauce, wine and beer will serve you well, as will dark earthy seasonings such as juniper, bay leaf, garlic and molasses. I'm a partisan of juniper and a splash of gin. In fact the odds are that you can guess a cook's national origin from their choice of meat accompaniments!

Remember that good cooking cannot change the quality of the meat itself. Carefully raised and butchered meat is pricey, especially beef and lamb which have been aged for greater tenderness and flavour, then properly trimmed. Provided you cook it correctly, it's much better to get the top grade of a cheaper cut than a cheap grade of a premium cut. Flank can rival fillet any day, but it must be treated right.

MIXED GRILL, PAGE 51

Large beef, lamb & game cuts Grilled, roasted

To add flavour to the tender cuts that lend themselves to grilling and roasting, you may want first to rub them with seasonings and/or herbs. Then refrigerate for an hour or two to allow the flavours to permeate. Add salt only at the last minute as this draws out juices. For crispness, sprinkle with flour. Score any fat and moisten the meat with a little oil so it browns well. To help smaller cuts start cooking rapidly, first brown them on the hob. During cooking, you must baste with pan drippings if roasting, or basting liquid, stock or wine if grilling. When done, let it stand in a warm place for at least 10 minutes.

COOKING METHODS FOR MEAT

Much depends on temperature: the high heat of roasting and grilling is simple and quick, but also dries meat, making no concessions to toughness, so you need to choose your cuts with care. By contrast, long slow cooking when you braise or stew meat with plenty of liquid has a moistening effect. With cuts suited to roasting, grilling or pan-frying, the outside is often seared so the juices caramelize and add flavour. Then the heat is allowed to penetrate to a greater or lesser degree (below). However, tougher cuts that should be braised, pot-roasted or boiled (poached) tolerate — indeed require — much longer cooking, so the slow moist heat breaks down tissue and tenderizes the meat.

THE FOUR STAGES IN ROASTING AND GRILLING MEAT:

• When underdone/blue, surface is hot but centre remains blue; texture is soft. Only beef steak and game such as ostrich are ever served this way.
• When rare, centre of meat starts to lose blue colour. Juices are pink and spurt when pierced. Tenderness at maximum, ideal for steak, lamb chops and most game, though old game may stay tough.
• When medium-cooked, heat reaches centre and meat is still very tender, though juices less pink.
• When well-done, meat stiffens and toughens. Centre is hot with no trace of pink juices. To avoid a dry chewy texture, do not go beyond this stage.

MEAT THERMOMETER READINGS FOR THE FOUR STAGES:
blue — thermometer registers less than 52°C/125°F.
rare — thermometer registers 52°C/125°F.
medium — thermometer registers 60°C/140°F.
well-done — thermometer registers 70°C/160°F.

ROASTING TIMES AND TEMPERATURES

Roasting temperature is a matter of debate, and I usually favour the French habit of starting with a very high heat of 230°C/450°F/gas8 for about 15 minutes until the meat is browned. After that, much depends on the size and type of meat. For a big cut I then turn down the heat to 175°C/350°F/gas4 to ensure the heat penetrates evenly to the centre of the meat. Approximate timings are: 12 minutes per 500 g/1 pound for underdone (blue) meat, 14-16 minutes per 500 g/1 pound for rare, 16-18 minutes per 500 g/1 pound for medium and 18-20 minutes per 500 g/1 pound for well-done meat. However, a plump cut takes longer and the long skinny shape of a beef fillet needs the highest possible heat for a short time.

TESTS FOR ROASTING

THERMOMETER – insert meat thermometer into the thickest part, without touching any bone, and allow at least 1 minute to register. Note: after being removed from oven, large cuts continue cooking for 5-10 minutes from their residual heat. Internal temperatures rise during this period, so take roast from the oven when just shy of right temperature.

SKEWER – insert metal skewer into thickest part of the meat, without touching any bone, and wait 30 seconds; if cold to the touch when withdrawn, meat is underdone; if cool, meat is rare; if warm, meat is medium-cooked; if hot, well done. Juices emerging when skewer is removed are red for rare meat, pink for medium-cooked and clear when meat is well-done. You'll also notice that rare meat clings to any bone, gradually pulling away during further cooking.

FINGERS – press or pinch with fingers. You'll learn difference between firm resilience of well-done meat and spongier feel of roast still rare in centre.

► **PERFECT BLUE** for beef and very lean game – surface browned but meat (here, beef fillet) still clings to any bone; surface of carved meat well-done, rest is rare to almost blue; juices not warm enough to run.

◄ **PERFECT RARE** for beef, lamb, buffalo, venison and ostrich – surface well browned, meat starting to pull from any bone; surface of carved meat well-done with centre red, very juicy and juices run red.

► **PERFECT MEDIUM** for beef, lamb, buffalo, venison – surface dark brown and meat shrinking from any bones; carved meat juicy, shading from crusty well-done surface to rose-pink centre; juices run deep pink.

◄ **PERFECT WELL-DONE** for beef, lamb, all game – surface crusty brown and whole roast visibly shrunken; when carved, meat has no trace of pink and surface is dry and fibrous; juices run clear.

Large cuts of veal Roasted

A veal roast calls for more delicate treatment than the red meats, though much of the advice on preparation, seasoning and basting holds true. You can choose between lightly roasted veal so it remains slightly pink, as I prefer, or veal roasted until well-done. Either way it's important not to let it overcook and become dry, so a longer time in the oven at a lower temperature is the wiser approach. I generally set the oven at 175°C/350°F/gas4, allowing about 20 minutes per 500 g/1 pound for medium-cooked and 2 minutes longer per 500 g/1 pound for well-done. Butter is the preferred basting fat for roast veal, both for flavour and because it helps brown the surface. Be sure the veal is tied compactly as it tends to shrink in the oven, and let it stand for at least 10 minutes before carving so the juices are redistributed. Overcooked and dry veal can be helped with generous amounts of butter or velouté sauce, or a rich gravy. Carving across the grain helps counteract toughness.

STAGES IN COOKING

▼ UNDERCOOKED – outside scarcely browned; skewer cool to touch when withdrawn after 30 seconds and juices run deep pink; thermometer registers less than 66°C/150°F; when carved, meat in centre is pink and translucent.

▲ PERFECT MEDIUM – outside of meat (here, rolled breast of veal stuffed with spinach and ricotta) is lightly browned; skewer is warm to the touch when withdrawn after 30 seconds and juices run lightly pink; meat thermometer registers 66°C/150°F; when carved, meat is juicy, slightly pink in centre and aromatic. Note: after being removed from oven, large cuts will continue cooking for 5-10 minutes from their own residual heat.

Large cuts of pork
Grilled, roasted

Pork must be cooked until well done (some pink juices are fine).
I use a moderately hot oven at 190°C/375°F/gas5, allowing 18
minutes per 500 g/1 pound for medium, or 20 minutes for well-done.
Best of all is the skin, often left on the roast and a prime part of
suckling pig. To help the skin dry and crisp, score it deeply, rub it with
salt and spices, and shortly after cooking begins, pour over a cup or
two of boiling water.

STAGES IN COOKING

▼ PERFECT WELL-DONE – outside
golden brown; when pressed, meat feels firm
(Thumb Test, fourth-finger stage, see page 52);
skewer is hot to touch when withdrawn after
30 seconds and juices run clear; meat
thermometer registers 70°C/160°F; when
carved, meat has no trace of pink but remains
juicy and full flavoured.

UNDERCOOKED ▶
– lightly browned and meat
(here, centre rib roast) clings
to bones; skewer cool or
warm after 30 seconds and
juices pink; thermometer less
than 70°C/160°F; carved,
meat pink in centre. Note:
cooking pork to 70-
75°C/160-170°F destroys
any possible trichinosis.

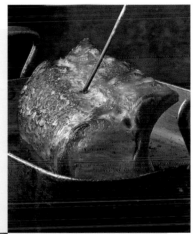

◀ PERFECT – well browned
and crusty, pulling away from
bones; thermometer 70°C/
160°F for medium-cooked, and
75°C/170°F for well-done;
skewer very warm or hot after
30 seconds and juices very
light pink (medium) or clear
(well-done); meat tender when
pierced; carved meat juicy and
with slight or no trace of pink.

Large beef, veal, lamb, pork & game cuts Boiled, braised, poached, pot-roasted

Compare the wide range of cuts that braise well with the few good for roasting and you'll see why I often say 'when in doubt, play safe and braise'. The truth is that most parts of an animal tend to be tough and benefit from slow moist heat to break down the tissue. There are no halfway measures for such meats – they must be cooked slowly and thoroughly until meltingly tender. Incidentally, the term 'boiled beef' is a misnomer; the key is to poach at a gentle simmer. The meat should always be brought slowly to the boil in cold liquid (usually water), then poached. If immersed in boiling liquid or simmered too fast, the surface will turn disagreeably hard. Salted meats such as brisket must be blanched before simmering. Before cooking, meat for braising or pot-roasting is often soaked in a wine or marinade, which is then used to make a sauce.

STAGES IN COOKING

▼ **PERFECT** – surface of meat (here, braised leg of lamb) moist, and brown if braised or pot-roasted; skewer hot to touch when withdrawn after 30 seconds and juices run clear; meat very tender when pierced, starting to pull from bones; thermometer registers 70°C/160°F; when sliced, meat is evenly cooked, moist and succulent.

▲ **PERFECT WELL-DONE** – surface of meat drier and very brown if braised or pot-roasted; skewer is very hot to the touch when withdrawn after 30 seconds; meat is soft enough to cut with a spoon and shrinks from bones; thermometer registers more than 70°C/160°F; when sliced, meat is very tender, almost falling into shreds.

Whole & half ham

Different types of ham call for quite different preparation, as hams vary far more than any other cut of meat. They may come raw or cooked, mild or salty, smoked or cured with a zesty pepper or spice mix. Strictly speaking, all hams are cut from the leg of pork, but today the term is often extended to include other cuts, such as pork shoulder. Don't be distracted by the term 'fresh ham' sometimes applied to fresh leg of pork.

Mildly cured and precooked hams are good cooked with very little liquid, baked or roasted in dry heat. Large cuts of bacon and gammon can be treated in the same way. On the other hand, well-aged or strongly cured hams, particularly those with a dry-salt cure, must first be soaked in water for 24 hours or longer, changing the water several times. Trim the skin, and to reduce fat, cut away all but a thin layer and then score it so it cooks evenly. Rather than being baked, braised, pot-roasted or roasted, such hams should be simmered in water with flavourings such as apple, onion, bay leaf and thyme (no salt). Note: if a ham is pallid or greyish, it is either not properly cured or stale. Don't use it.

▲ **PERFECT** – meat starting to shrink from bone and bone feels loose; skewer is hot to the touch when withdrawn after 30 seconds; thermometer registers 75°C/170°F; if baked, braised, pot-roasted or roasted, surface is scored and well browned with a caramelized glaze; when carved, meat is juicy and clear or deep pink, depending on cure; flavour vigorous but not salty.

Steaks, lamb chops & game medallions

Grilled, fried, sautéed

Steaks and lamb chops are by far the most popular meats in any cook's repertoire. Medallions and noisettes, small tender pieces which are easy to cook, are equally sought after when it comes to game. My instinct is to cook such luxury cuts very simply as in the Mixed Grill opposite, adding at most a pat of herb butter. Top-quality meat, marbled with plenty of fat for beef and lamb, is essential for successful grilling and pan-frying. Unfortunately, there are few cuts tender enough to withstand such dry heat, and they are normally expensive. Remember that beef and game can be very dry if well done. See also Stages in roasting and grilling meat, on page 44.

STAGES IN COOKING

▼ **PERFECT RARE** for beef, lamb and game – well-browned and spongy in centre when pressed (Thumb Test, 2nd-finger stage, page 52), firm at sides; beads of juice deep pink.

▲ **PERFECT UNDERDONE AND BLUE** for beef – surface seared and meat (here, steak) offers no resistance when pressed (Thumb Test, first-finger stage, page 52); beads of meat juice not yet risen to surface; when cut, meat is rare to almost blue, flavour mild.

▲ **PERFECT MEDIUM** for beef, lamb and game – surface crusty brown and meat resists when centre pressed (Thumb Test, 3rd-finger stage, page 52), firm at sides; beads of juice on surface are pink; when cut, meat is juicy, deep pink and well-flavoured.

Mixed grill

Mix this grill to suit your tastes and what's best at the butcher's.

SERVES 4

4 small fillet steaks (about 500 g/1 pound)
4 lamb rib chops (about 375 g/³⁄₄ pound)
4 small slices of veal liver (about 500 g/1 pound)
4 chestnut mushrooms (about 375 g/³⁄₄ pound)
2 tomatoes, cored and halved

45 g/1¹⁄₂ oz melted butter, more if needed
bunch of watercress, for decoration

FOR THE PARSLEY BUTTER
1 tablespoon chopped parsley
1 teaspoon lemon juice
75 g/2¹⁄₂ oz butter, softened
salt and pepper

First make the parsley butter: beat the parsley and lemon juice into the butter. Season. Wrap in a cylinder in cling film and chill.

Preheat the grill. Brush the mushrooms and tomato halves on both sides with some melted butter and season. Brush the grill rack with more melted butter. Put the mushrooms and tomatoes on the rack, setting the tomatoes cut side down. Grill about 7.5 cm/3 inches from the heat, turning the tomatoes once, until just tender, 4-5 minutes on each side. Brush the mushrooms occasionally with butter and grill until tender, 5-7 minutes on each side. Transfer to a serving platter and keep warm.

Brush the steaks, chops and liver with melted butter and season. Set the steak and chops on the rack and grill, turning once, until done to taste, 3-4 minutes per side for rare meat, 4-5 minutes for medium-cooked and 6-8 minutes for well-done. After 2-3 minutes, add the liver to the rack and grill, turning once, until done to your taste, 3-4 minutes on each side.

Unwrap the chilled parsley butter, slice across into rounds and set two or three on each steak. Decorate with watercress.

▼ **PERFECT WELL-DONE** for beef, lamb and game – surface crusty brown and dry; meat firm when pressed in centre (Thumb Test, 4th-finger stage, page 52); beads of juice on surface clear.

Veal chops, medallions & small cuts

Grilled, fried, sautéed

The tenderness and delicate flavour of veal show best in small cuts like chops and medallions, provided they are simply cooked. The main danger is dryness, so before frying or grilling, I often brush veal generously with oil or, even better, marinate it in olive or walnut oil flavoured with lemon juice or balsamic vinegar and herbs. For another approach, coat veal with flour to help retain juices and keep the surface of the meat crisp.

STAGES IN COOKING

PERFECT MEDIUM ▶
– surface lightly browned and meat (here, medallions) spongy when pressed in centre, firm at sides (Thumb Test, 2nd-finger stage, right); beads of juice on surface pink; when cut, meat is juicy, faintly pink and aromatic.

◀ PERFECT WELL-DONE
– surface golden brown, crusty if grilled; meat firm when pressed in centre (Thumb Test, 4th-finger stage, right); beads of juice on surface clear; when cut, no pink juices visible but meat still moist and well-flavoured.

THUMB TEST FOR FIRMNESS

As this is such a simple way to judge the cooking of a piece of meat, as well as fish (see page 21) and poultry, I am repeating it here. The idea is to compare the food's resilience to that of your thumb muscle. The further the thumb has to reach across the hand, the more resilient the muscle becomes.

FIRST-FINGER STAGE

for underdone/blue meat – touch your thumb to its opposing first finger and press the ball of your thumb with the tip of a finger of the other hand – the ball will offer no resistance.

SECOND-FINGER STAGE

for rare meat – touch your second finger to your thumb and press the ball – it will feel spongy.

THIRD-FINGER STAGE

for medium-cooked meat or game – touch your third finger to your thumb and press the ball of your thumb – the ball will feel resistant.

FOURTH-FINGER STAGE

for well-done meat – touch your fourth finger to your thumb and press the ball – it will feel firm.

Steaks, chops and game pieces

Baked, braised, stewed

Braising, baking or stewing are the ways to go with beef brisket and back ribs, with less expensive steaks from the round, chuck or blade, together with lamb shoulder chops, neck slices, riblets and shanks, and game leg or shoulder slices and shanks – all boneless or on the bone. It's also safest for most small pieces of wild game as only the best cuts of farmed venison can be relied upon to be tender if grilled. The advantages of cooking in moist heat are many, but cooking must be sufficiently slow to allow the meat fibres to soften and relax. Prior marinating of the meat also helps both texture and flavour.

▶ **PERFECT VEAL ESCALOPES** – lightly browned on both sides; when cut, meat is white and juicy with no trace of pink.

▼ **PERFECT** – meat (here, braised rump steak) very tender, pulling from bone and falling easily from a two-pronged fork; meat is moist and very well flavoured, with tender gelatinous tissue.

ESCALOPES

When escalopes are mentioned, veal is generally understood, but slices from turkey and chicken breasts are gaining ground as inexpensive alternatives. Many recipes advise flattening escalopes between sheets of paper, but be gentle; if you pound them to pieces, they will lose all their juices. They need equally delicate cooking as they overcook in minutes. The best veal escalopes are cut from the round; for tenderness, they should be sliced across the grain with little or no seam of connective tissue. Watch out for cheaper imitations from less desirable veal cuts as they are liable to be stringy.

Pork chops, spare ribs & ham steaks

The pork we eat today is considerably leaner than even 10 years ago. Less fat means less protection in cooking, so it's no surprise that chops and other lean cuts like medallions or fillet slices are often best braised or stewed. I like my pork thoroughly cooked, while recognizing that the meat should remain tender and full of its natural juices. However, lighter cooking is quite acceptable. In any case, pork does well on the bone, one reason why spare ribs are so popular, and so delicious. Spare ribs call for creative basting sauces such as the spicy Classic Barbecue Sauce opposite, or an Oriental mix of soy sauce, brown sugar and rice wine. The same combinations are also good with a thick ham steak, as spicy flavours complement the salty cure. Much depends on the ham and if it is strongly cured, you may want to soak it in cold water to leach out some salt before cooking. If ham does still end up being oversalty, balance this by serving it with a fruit sauce such as plum or apple; if it is really very salty, use it in soup, or to flavour pasta, rice or potatoes.

STAGES IN COOKING

▼ **UNDERCOOKED** – surface lightly browned and meat (here, pork chops) clings to bone; when cut with a knife, meat is very pink; beads of juice on surface are pink; meat is firm at sides, spongy in centre when pressed with a fingertip (Thumb Test, 2nd-finger stage, page 52). Note: cooking pork to 70-75°C/160-170°F destroys any possible trichinosis.

▲ **PERFECT** – surface browned (especially pork) and meat starting to pull from bone; when cut, meat is juicy; beads of juice on surface are very light pink when medium-cooked or clear for well-done; for medium-cooked, meat is firm at sides and centre resists when pressed (Thumb Test, 3rd-finger stage, see page 52); when well-done, meat firm at sides and centre when pressed (4th-finger stage).

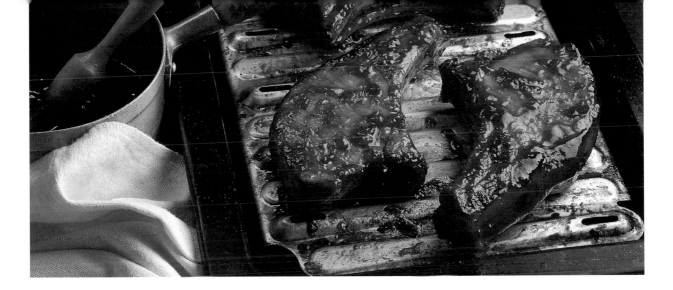

Grilled pork chops with classic barbecue sauce

**Constant basting with this lively sauce ensures moist chops and plenty of flavour. A
warm potato salad is the natural accompaniment.**

SERVES 4

**4 pork loin chops (about 250 g/¹/₂
   pound each), cut 2.5 cm/I inch thick
salt and pepper**

FOR THE CLASSIC BARBECUE SAUCE

**2 tablespoons vegetable oil
I onion, finely chopped
I garlic clove, fincly chopped
I lemon
100 g/3¹/₄ oz brown sugar
60 ml/2 fl oz vinegar
125 ml/4 fl oz tomato ketchup
I tablespoon Worcestershire sauce
¹/₂ teaspoon Tabasco sauce, or to taste
¹/₄ teaspoon chilli powder, or to taste**

Make the barbecue sauce: heat the oil in a frying pan and
sauté the onion and garlic until soft and lightly browned,
4-5 minutes. Grate the zest from the lemon and squeeze
the juice. Add the lemon zest, half the lemon juice, the
sugar, vinegar, ketchup, Worcestershire sauce, Tabasco sauce
and chilli powder to the onion and simmer gently,
5 minutes. Taste, adjust the seasoning and let cool.

Preheat the grill or light the barbecue. Season the pork
chops with salt and pepper and brush with the cooled
barbecue sauce. Grill them, basting often, 5-7 minutes. Turn
over and continue grilling and basting until the chops are
done, 5-7 minutes longer.

Meat stews

In a good stew, flavours are intense, the result not just of good seasoning but also of long simmering and reduction of the cooking liquid. If the meat is first to be browned, do so thoroughly, then add the toughest vegetables first so that everything finishes cooking at the same time; use herbs and spices generously. What makes a stew special is not the meat itself, but the way all the other ingredients have been blended into a perfect sauce. A stew provides a chance to use all of those odd pieces – ribs, breast, flank, shank, etc. If meat is on the bone, as with ribs, veal shank or neck, flavour is all the more intense. When choosing meat for a stew don't be put off by sinew, or a bit of fat. Well-marbled beef or lamb will be all the more tasty and tender, and exterior fat can be trimmed off to taste. Sinew dissolves after lengthy cooking, turning meltingly tender and adding rich gelatine to the sauce. Whenever you can, I would advise first marinating meat for stews.

STAGES IN COOKING

▼ TOUGH AND UNDERCOOKED – meat pieces resist when pinched between finger and thumb and cling to a two-pronged fork; sauce is thin, lacking flavour.

▲ PERFECT – when pinched between finger and thumb, meat crushes with little resistance; meat pieces are tender and fall easily when pierced with a two-pronged fork; meat is well-browned (for beef, lamb and game), or lightly browned or white (for pork and veal); sauce is rich, glossy and aromatic.

Minced meats

Minced meat must be freshly prepared as it starts to deteriorate within 12 hours even when tightly wrapped in the refrigerator. The justification for mincing meat is to render tough pieces palatable, so a relatively inexpensive cut is fine provided it has no sinew and little fat. If possible, mince the meat yourself in a traditional mincer (a food processor pounds rather than cuts fibres and will make the meat heavy).

▼ **OVERCOOKED** – pieces are soft, starting to fall apart; sauce is muddy, with fat separated on surface.

STAGES IN COOKING

PERFECT LIGHTLY COOKED ▶
– (not suitable for pork and see note on page 47) – if dry-cooked, surface crusty brown and beads of juices on surface pink; if simmered or stewed, surface brown and moist; when pressed, centre spongy, edges firm (Thumb Test, second-finger stage, see page 52), centre slightly resistant.

◀ PERFECT WELL-DONE
– if dry-cooked, surface crusty, slightly charred, and beads of juice on surface clear; if simmered or stewed, surface well browned and moist; when pressed, both centre and edges are firm (Thumb Test, fourth-finger stage, see page 52).

Meat terrines

Don't think of terrines as merely a fancy french affair; plain meat loaves belong to the same family. All are a wonderful way to dress up various minced meats. Pork, including pork liver, is the top choice for richness, with beef and game runners-up for flavour; veal or chicken add delicacy, but can be dry. Only lamb is off limits as in a terrine it tends to taste unpleasantly strong. Careful cooking of a terrine or meat loaf is as important as the quality of the mixture itself. To help the heat spread evenly, use a heavy mould and oil it or line it with barding fat or bacon to keep the contents moist. Delicate terrines are sealed with a flour-and-water paste and then baked in the oven in a water bath (the water must be brought to the boil on the hob first so cooking time can be estimated accurately). To make a terrine easier to slice, press it with a weight as it cools. More robust loaves can be baked uncovered so they form a crisp brown crust; they do not need pressing.

STAGES IN COOKING

UNDERCOOKED ▼
– mixture soft in centre when pressed; a skewer inserted in centre is cool or warm when withdrawn after 30 seconds; meat thermometer inserted in centre registers less than 75°C/170°F; juices pink; when cut, texture wet and flabby.

◄ PERFECT
– mixture shrinks from sides of mould and is firm when pressed; a skewer inserted in centre is hot when withdrawn after 30 seconds; thermometer inserted in centre registers 75°C/170°F; juices run clear not pink; when cut, texture is firm and moist.

► DRY AND OVERCOOKED –
shrunken, surrounded by melted fat and juices; skewer inserted in centre is very hot when removed after 30 seconds; thermometer registers more than 75°C/170°F; when cut, terrine is dry, crumbling on outside.

Mushroom-sage meatloaf

Minced meat that is served hot, such as in meatloaf, take less seasoning than terrines and other cold mixtures. Mashed potatoes make the perfect accompaniment to this meatloaf.

SERVES 6-8

900 g/2 pounds minced beef
450 g/1 pound minced pork
6 slices of white bread, crusts discarded
125 ml/4 fl oz milk
1 tablespoon vegetable oil, more for the pan
15 g/1/2 oz butter
1 large onion, chopped
175 g/6 oz button mushrooms, chopped
1 garlic clove, chopped
4 tablespoons chopped fresh sage
2 tablespoons Worcestershire sauce

3 eggs, beaten, to mix
2 teaspoons salt
1/2 teaspoon pepper
250 ml/8 fluid ounces double cream, for the
   sauce

FOR THE TOPPING

1 tablespoon Dijon mustard
1 tablespoon brown sugar
6 slices of bacon

23x12.5-cm/9x5-inch loaf pan

Preheat the oven to 175°C/350°F/gas4 and oil the loaf pan. In a large bowl, mix together the beef and pork. Tear the bread into crumbs with your fingers, put it in another bowl and mix in the milk.

Heat the oil and butter in a medium frying pan. Add the onions and fry them over medium heat until soft but not brown, 5-7 minutes. Stir in the mushrooms, cover and cook them until they have released their juices, 3-5 minutes. Remove the lid, increase the heat and cook, stirring, until this liquid has evaporated. Take from the heat and stir in the chopped garlic, sage and Worcestershire sauce.

Using a wooden spoon, stir the mushroom mixture into the meats together with the soaked breadcrumbs, eggs, salt and pepper. Stir gently until the mixture holds together, but do not overwork or the meatloaf will be tough. Fry a small ball of the mixture in the frying pan. Taste it and adjust the seasoning of the remaining mixture if necessary. Spoon the mixture into the oiled loaf pan, packing it well and mounding it slightly in the centre.

Make the topping by stirring the mustard with the sugar and spreading this over the top of the loaf. Lay the bacon slices diagonally across the meat. Bake in the oven for about 1 1/4 – 1 1/2 hours until a skewer inserted in the centre is hot to the touch when withdrawn after 30 seconds. The loaf should be firm to the touch and the juices should run clear. A meat thermometer inserted in the centre should register 70°C/160°F. Remove from the oven and let it sit for 15 minutes.

Pour the juices from the meatloaf into a small saucepan and spoon off most of the fat. Boil the juices until they are reduced by half, 5-8 minutes. Pour in the cream and boil until reduced and thickened, another 5-8 minutes. Take the sauce from the heat, whisk in the Dijon mustard, taste and adjust the seasoning. Slice the meatloaf and arrange these overlapping on a platter. Serve the sauce separately.

Vegetables

There's more to the humble vegetable than meets the eye. Living at Château du Feÿ, with a vegetable garden in full production, has been a revelation. Every year is different, with tomatoes a bumper crop one season, yet the next they scarcely manage to ripen. Leeks seem to flourish no matter what the weather, but garlic and shallots are timid and supply is always meagre. I've learned that produce varies also with the seasons – the same potatoes which are firm and waxy when first harvested, have dried six months later to the floury consistency that is perfect for purée.

The point is that cooking vegetables is not a matter of standard rules. Instructions on seasoning, cooking methods and timing can never be more than approximate. Therefore, being able to recognize when a vegetable is cooked just right is doubly important. In this chapter I've deliberately concentrated on tricky varieties such as asparagus, which is inedibly chewy if underdone but can overcook in a moment or two. Greens have at least two useful stages of cooking, blanched and lightly cooked. Roots, also, can be cooked until just tender, but if they are to be puréed or used for soup they must be very soft. Onions change flavour radically depending on how fast and how long they are cooked and whether or not they are allowed to brown and caramelize.

The vegetable tribe is so varied that only a few universal rules hold good. Some vegetables discolour easily when peeled, notably roots such as potato and celeriac, white asparagus, and globe artichokes, so cut them with a stainless-steel knife and if necessary hold them in water acidulated with lemon juice. There's a move towards leaving the peel on vegetables both for flavour and nutrients, but be aware that fertilizers and pesticides also collect near the surface. In this case, organically grown produce is a good idea. When preparing vegetables, cut them in even-sized pieces so they cook evenly as well as look attractive.

This is just a beginning. I've learned so much more from the chefs at La Varenne. It was Chef Chambrette who introduced me to his buttered cabbage, made by blanching cabbage then slowly baking it with quantities of butter until it falls into a glistening rich confit. Pumpkin soup was Chef Claude's speciality – the whole pumpkin was filled with milk and baked in its skin until the flesh could be scooped out with a spoon, leaving a spectacular serving container. Demonstrations by Chef Bouvier introduced me to clouds of deep-fried ginger and leek julienne as a garnish for fish. Giant bouquets of herbs appeared in the kitchen, a reflection of the huge amounts which infuse contemporary cuisine.

GLAZED ROOT VEGETABLES, PAGE 85

Artichokes

A boiled artichoke is a conundrum, its prickles and hairy choke bristling guardians of the rich flesh inside. I do so appreciate a cook who trims an artichoke before cooking, snapping the stem, trimming the top with a knife and snipping spines from the leaves. When cooking artichokes, keep the water at a steady simmer and allow at least 1 litre/1⅔ pints of salted water per artichoke. A single garlic clove pushed inside the leaves perfumes the whole artichoke and a squeeze of lemon juice in the water helps preserve the green colour. Artichokes tend to float during cooking, acquiring an ugly 'tide mark' at water level, so I sink them firmly with a heavy heatproof plate. Young artichokes cook in 20-30 minutes, but when large and mature they can take up to an hour. Artichokes that have been cooked without being properly trimmed are often quite bitter; you can disguise this with a tart lemon vinaigrette.

STAGES IN COOKING

► **PERFECT** – artichoke even olive green colour; leaf pulled from near centre comes out easily; heart tender when pierced; flavour rich, intense but not bitter.

▼ **OVERCOOKED AND DRAB** – leaves falling from artichoke; centre very soft when pierced; colour muddy.

PREVENTING DISCOLORATION

Like many fruits, several types of vegetable oxidize readily when peeled or cut, and the flesh exposed to the air will discolour dramatically. When preparing such vegetables, like artichokes, potatoes, parsnips, celeriac, Jerusalem artichokes, salsify and avocados, it is preferable to use a stainless steel knife, as contact with other types of metal can exacerbate the situation.

Acids like vinegar or lemon juice will prevent oxidation, so as soon as the vegetable is cut either rub any exposed surfaces of the vegetable with a cut lemon or brush it all over with vinegar or lemon juice. Root vegetables should immediately be immersed in cold water; for potatoes this is sufficient, but other roots need the water to be acidulated with a dash of vinegar or lemon juice. It is also a good idea idea to add vinegar or lemon juice to the cooking water.

Asparagus

Asparagus appears in two guises – green and white. The most succulent size for green asparagus is a matter of debate. Personally I think it is at its best quite slim, particularly as very thin spears really do not need to be peeled. White asparagus, grown under the ground so the stems stay blanched, is another matter. Here the fatter the spears the better. They must always be peeled to remove the outer, woody skin, and even then you will sometimes run across fibrous white asparagus which cannot be made tender by thorough boiling. In this case, use the stems for soup, reserving the tips for garnish. Asparagus is usually boiled in salted water, either blanched (page 69) for a salad or stir-fry, or lightly cooked as shown below. Asparagus can also be grilled, first brushing it with oil or melted butter so it does not dry out.

STAGES IN COOKING

▼ PERFECT BLANCHED
– spears bend just slightly when lifted and are resistant when poked with a knife; texture is slightly crunchy but not fibrous; colour is vivid green.

OVERCOOKED ▼
– spears are floppy when lifted and soft when poked with a knife; texture is soft, even slippery; colour tinged with yellow.

▲ PERFECT LIGHTLY COOKED
– spears bend when lifted and are just tender when poked with knife; texture firm but not crunchy, and colour a clear green; flavour fresh with no grassy overtones. Spears can vary in size; if necessary, sort and tie them by size so thin stems which cook more quickly can be removed first.

Stalks & shoots

Stalks and shoots such as celery, chicory, cardoon, chard, fennel and leeks turn up in many guises all over the world and several are edible raw. Where would Italy be without fennel, or China without bamboo shoots? Not necessarily related botanically, stalks and shoots share much in common in the kitchen. They are robust and crisp, lending themselves to a variety of cooking methods, from braising to grilling to steaming. However, many have a fibrous texture which is aggravated by improper cooking and they will turn tasteless or bitter if overcooked. These staple vegetables provide many favourite dishes, such as celery soup, braised chicory with ham in cheese sauce, leek vinaigrette and Italian fennel braised in milk. Tasty stalks like celery, leek and fennel also turn up in flavouring mixtures for soups and braises, often combined with onion, carrot and herbs.

STAGES IN COOKING

▼ **PERFECT BLANCHED** – vegetable opaque; crisp when poked with a knife; texture crunchy, slightly fibrous and flavour grassy. Note: some stalks and shoots, such as fennel and chicory, are edible after blanching (page 69), but others like leek and chard need further cooking.

▲ **PERFECT** – vegetable slightly translucent; just tender when pierced with point of a knife, but holding shape well; flavour full-bodied.

Green beans, sugar snap & mange-tout peas

Controversy rages over the cooking of green beans. One school of thought likes them blanched (page 69), still crunchy. The other, to which I subscribe, maintains that crunchy green beans taste too grassy and need 1-2 additional minutes cooking to develop their flavour fully. Take your pick! All cooks reunite on sugar snap and mange-tout peas, whose pods become slippery and fall apart when overcooked. Brief cooking is essential here and one minute can make the difference between a mange-tout pea that's just right, and one gone too far. Don't forget that beans and pea pods have tops, stems and often strings that must be removed before cooking. Being tricky to boil, mange-tout peas are popular crisply stir-fried. To ensure sugar snap peas live up to their name, I think they are best simply boiled or steamed, then tossed perhaps in a little butter.

STAGES IN COOKING

▼ **PERFECT BLANCHED** – still crisp enough to snap (here, string beans); slightly softened but crunchy, resistant to knife; flavour grassy, not fully developed; use blanched peas and beans in stir-fries and add to soups, sautés and stews.

▲ **PERFECT** – tender enough to bend but still slightly crisp; easy to cut with knife; colour vivid and taste well-defined and fresh.

Broccoli & cauliflower

From the cooking viewpoint, broccoli and cauliflower have two parts, the stem and the more delicate floret. There's no problem with trimmed florets, but when stem is included (and it's good) it must be pared down to cook as rapidly as the floret. Like most Englishwomen, I was brought up on cauliflower cheese and I much appreciate the modern version which includes broccoli. The Italian alternative of broccoli sautéed in olive oil and garlic is pretty tasty too, as is cauliflower in Spanish style with a garlic and paprika sauce. Boiled or steamed broccoli and cauliflower that are slightly overcooked can be partially rescued by spreading them carefully on a baking sheet and drying them for 3-5 minutes in a low oven.

STAGES IN COOKING

▼ **PERFECT BLANCHED** – stem resistant when poked with point of a knife and texture slightly crunchy; colour virtually unchanged; ideal for salads, stir-frying and serving in crudités.

▲ **PERFECT** – stem is just tender when pierced with point of a knife; cut stems are slightly translucent, with florets still intact; colour vivid green or white, texture firm and just short of crunchy; flavour fresh.

Green peas, sweetcorn kernels

Though belonging to quite different botanical families, green peas and corn kernels are cooked alike. When boiling or steaming them, follow the guidelines for green vegetables (see Blanching and boiling green vegetables, page 69). Baby peas are still at their best quite plainly boiled, although they also make a memorable soup. When older and tougher, I prefer to braise them, possibly with ham. With sweetcorn, quality is all-important – it must be young and freshly picked. If in doubt, add sugar instead of salt to water for boiling, or include garlic cloves when roasting.

◄ PERFECT BLANCHED – texture crunchy but skins softened somewhat; colours vivid, flavours undeveloped. Add to stir-fries, sautés and stews.

► PERFECT – corn or peas are just tender, still slightly chewy; colours are vivid and flavours fresh.

◄ OVERCOOKED AND SOFT – texture mushy and skins often bursting; fresh colour and flavour lost.

CORN ON THE COB

Every few years our garden produces a bumper crop of corn, and we delight in eating it with plenty of butter. Peeling off the husk and pulling away the silk is easy, and then in the pot of boiling water it goes. To roast or grill the ears in the husk, strip it back, remove the silk, brush the corn with butter or oil and seasoning and rewrap in the husk. An unpeeled garlic clove and a sprinkling of red pepper oil adds zip and you'll know when the corn is done by the fragrant aroma. When corn is elderly, no amount of cooking will make it tender, so cut it from the cob to add to soup or a salad. Perfectly cooked kernels can be prised easily from cob with the point of a knife; they will be tender but still slightly chewy with juicy, sweet flavour.

Hearty greens including spinach & cabbage

If they are fibrous, it's a good idea to soften greens which are old or tough by blanching before cooking them further (slicing greens across the fibres helps minimize toughness). Blanching also tempers bitterness and helps set bright colour (see opposite). Spinach and green and white cabbage are the most versatile of the group, while more robust greens such as mustard, collards and red cabbage are best baked, braised or stewed to mellow their brash flavours. Red cabbage must always be cooked with vinegar or another acid ingredient to set its cheerful colour.

STAGES IN COOKING

▼ **PERFECT BLANCHED** – colour vivid; greens softened but still very crunchy; resistant to the knife; flavour grassy and not fully developed.

▼ **OVERCOOKED AND SOFT** – leaves limp and watery; colour yellowed or muddy and flavour flat, sometimes sour.

▲ **PERFECT** – colour still bright (here, cabbage); when boiled, sautéed, steamed or sweated, greens tender and translucent (for cabbage, chicory and escarole) but slightly crunchy, easy to cut with a knife; flavour well defined and fresh; when baked, braised or stewed, greens are tender, moist but not watery and easy to cut with a spoon, but not chewy; flavour is full-bodied and rich.

Lettuce & salad greens

Not until I lived with a vegetable garden did I realize the reason for cooking the delicate greens that are usually eaten raw in a salad. The annual cascade of overgrown, chewy lettuce about to bolt has led generations of cooks to save its life by braising, steaming or shredding lettuce to simmer as a surprisingly piquant soup. Flavour, never very strong in salad greens, gets a boost in dishes such as braised Boston or Cos lettuce with sliced onion, carrots and ham, or sautéed escarole or frisée with onion, lemon juice, coriander and paprika. Recently, grilled greens, particularly radicchio, have become popular, at their best basted with a simple mix of virgin olive oil, salt and cracked black pepper. The key to cooking salad greens is to tenderize them (they can be quite stringy) without losing their pretty colour.

STAGES IN COOKING

▶ **PERFECT BLANCHED** – colour brilliant; texture wilted but still crispy, resistant to the knife; flavour still grassy. Blanching sets colour and helps remove bitterness before further cooking.

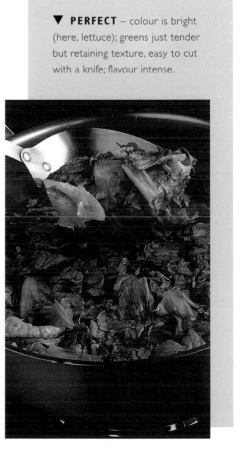

▼ **PERFECT** – colour is bright (here, lettuce); greens just tender but retaining texture, easy to cut with a knife; flavour intense.

BLANCHING AND BOILING GREENS

Green vegetables are blanched for several reasons: to set their colour, to temper strong flavour or to soften a hard or fibrous texture. Boiling, by contrast, implies that the vegetable will be fully (albeit lightly) cooked. When boiling green vegetables there's an ancient rule of thumb: put them into boiling water and cook them as rapidly as possible, uncovered. This treatment, in fact, best preserves their vitamin content and fragile cellular structure; leaving the vegetables uncovered allows acids to vaporize which would otherwise turn them yellow. Be sure vegetables are cut into even pieces. Boil rapidly to the stage wanted, then drain and immerse or rinse in cold water to stop cooking instantly, so as much bright green colour as possible is retained.

Summer & winter squash including courgette & pumpkin

Summer squash belies its name and brightens our plates for most of the year. The family includes crookneck, cucumber, vegetable marrow, pattypan, scallop, yellow squash and courgette. It's best to leave these soft-fleshed vegetables unpeeled, both for colour and to hold them together. Small size is important as overgrown summer squash bloat with water and lose flavour. Given so much moisture, they overcook easily, so avoid slicing thinly unless they are to be cooked rapidly by deep- or stir-frying. Mature summer squash also develop large seeds, best scooped out and discarded. Decorative miniature squash are one way of guaranteeing firm texture, though they can be bitter.

STAGES IN COOKING

▼ **PERFECT BLANCHED** – colour bright, still opaque; texture moist and slightly crunchy. Served as crudités, used in salads and stir-fries.

▼ **OVERCOOKED AND WET** – colour faded, texture watery and very soft when pierced with point of knife; pieces often collapsed and very dark brown; flavour insipid. Note: summer squash overcook very easily, often in a minute or two.

▲ **PERFECT LIGHTLY COOKED** – translucent, just tender when pierced with a knife, firm but not crunchy; colour vivid and edges lightly browned; flavour fresh for summer squash, smooth for winter types. Note: squash for soup or purée should be very tender, but not so soft as to be watery.

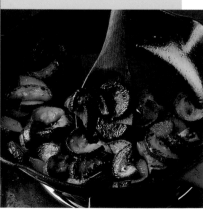

Aubergines

Vegetarian cooking without aubergine is unimaginable, so robust and meaty is its texture. During cooking, aubergine has the curious habit of absorbing liquid or fat like a sponge, then expelling it when the flesh shrinks under heat. It helps to salt aubergine before cooking by halving or slicing the flesh, then sprinkling it with salt to draw out moisture. Leave 15-30 minutes, then rinse and drain before continuing with the recipe. Sprinkling with salt can also counteract bitterness in mature aubergine (large seeds are a bad sign). If your cooked aubergine is bland, or in the unlikely event of it becoming overcooked and dry, brush it lightly with olive oil, then combine or layer with juicy ingredients such as tomato, fried onion, white or cheese sauce, or meat sauce as in moussaka. A sprinkling of grated cheese hides more shortcomings. Alternatively, sprinkle aubergine Turkish-style with cumin seeds, lemon juice, cayenne, chopped mint and a little sugar.

STAGES IN COOKING

▼ **PERFECT LIGHTLY COOKED** – with or without skin, aubergine flesh is juicy and meltingly tender, somewhat translucent and lightly browned; flavour is rich, almost smoky.

▲ **PERFECT CRISP** – deep golden crisp on outside, but still soft in centre; flavour is rich, smoky and sweet.

Sweet peppers & chillies

For the cook, the capsicum pepper family falls into two groups: sweet peppers, and hot peppers (chillies). Within these two categories, botanists identify hundreds of different kinds, their flavours depending not just on variety, but also on the soil in which they have been grown. So peppers are to some extent a lottery – you must taste and try. Flavour is also much altered when a pepper is roasted or grilled, charring the skin so it can then be peeled off, leaving only the tender flesh for a salad or for chopping or puréeing for a sauce. For crunchy texture, you can leave peppers unpeeled before chopping or slicing. When baking with a stuffing, peppers are often left unpeeled so they hold their shape better. Blanching is a halfway house, a way to soften the peppers and moderate their sometimes sharp taste.

STAGES IN COOKING

▼ **PERFECT WHOLE PEPPERS FOR PEELING** – if grilled or roasted, skin charred and flesh limp but still firm, juicy and colourful with smoky taste; if stuffed and baked or roasted in skin, still holding a shape but tender when poked with a knife.

▼ **OVERCOOKED AND WET** – peppers are limp, faded and bland.

▲ **PERFECT BLANCHED** – colour vivid and texture lightly crisp, resistant when pierced with knife; flavour slightly grassy. Blanched peppers, particularly strips, are used in salads and for decoration.

Tomatoes

We use tomatoes so often fresh in salad or mixed with other vegetables that it's easy to overlook them as a cooked vegetable in their own right. When you cook a tomato thoroughly, its flavour will change radically, losing its fruity tartness and mellowing to be rich and concentrated. Tomatoes often need to be peeled and blanching makes this easy. Bring a large pan of water to the boil. Cut out the cores and mark a small cross in the flower end of each tomato. Plunge them into boiling water and leave until the skin pulls away from the cross, 10 seconds or longer if the tomatoes are not very ripe. Transfer to cold water and peel when cool (see below left). Remember that, when cooking tomatoes, it often helps to add a teaspoon of sugar – tomatoes are, after all, a fruit.

STAGES IN COOKING

▼ PERFECT BLANCHED FOR PEELING
– skin pulls away from tomato and is very easy to peel; flesh is still uncooked and firm.

▲ PERFECT BAKED – tomato hot, juicy, tender when pierced with point of a knife, but still holding shape; skin starting to split; colour vivid, flavour assertive.

Potatoes Baked, braised, steamed, boiled

Common white-fleshed potatoes fall into two groups: firm, waxy varieties which hold their shape during cooking; and floury or baking potatoes which purée easily. Waxy potatoes are good for boiling, steaming, sautéing or simmering in liquid, when the potato needs to stay firm. When boiling potatoes, remember to start them out in cold water (as with other root vegetables). Cover the pan, bring to the boil and simmer, so the potato cooks gently without falling apart. Waxy potatoes are right for potato salad; floury potatoes are good for everything else – for baking in the oven, for mashing, for deep-frying, for roast potatoes cooked to accompany a roast, and for baking in liquid to melting tenderness as a gratin. The limited selection of potatoes in the average market gives little clue to their diversity. We're seeing more and more 'boutique' potatoes, perhaps coloured a dusky purple or pink, or in odd shapes like the cylindrical French la ratte. Most behave like standard potatoes, whether waxy or floury, but have flavour superior to the average supermarket varieties.

▶ UNDERCOOKED – potato hard when pierced with point of a knife;

When cut, centre is translucent.

▶ PERFECT – tender but doesn't break up when pierced.

When cut, potato opaque. Cook steamed/boiled potatoes and those to be served in sauce to this stage.

**▶ PERFECT
WELL-COOKED** –
skin peels easily and
outside floury.

Potato very tender,
almost falling apart.
Cook baked
potatoes and those
steamed/boiled for
puréeing to this
stage

▶ OVERCOOKED –
very floury; water-
logged if cooked in
liquid, shrivelled if
baked;

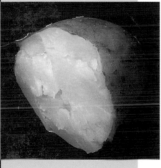

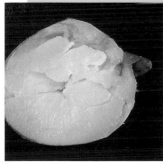

Potato very soft
and disintegrating.
You can recover
those cooked in
liquid slightly by
drying in low oven.

MASHED POTATOES

With its soft texture and adaptable taste, the
potato is the ideal vegetable for mashing and
puréeing. For a classic potato purée, rich yet fluffy
and falling easily from the spoon, the guidelines are
clear. First choose the right floury type of potato
(see opposite). Cut into even 2.5-cm/1-inch chunks.
(I leave the peel as it adds flavour and helps hold
the potato together during cooking.) Immediately
immerse potatoes in a pan of cold salted water,
cover and bring to the boil. Simmer until very
tender when pierced with a knife, 15-20 minutes,
then drain. Let cool slightly and remove skin. To dry,
warm gently in the pan or spread on a baking sheet
in a low oven.

    Potatoes are full of starch and the aim when
puréeing is to expand and fluff the grains without
letting them glue together. Work the potatoes
through a ricer or a coarse strainer, or simply mash
thoroughly in the pan. To lighten and smooth the
purée, it is beaten over heat with a wooden spoon,
adding hot milk or cream and generous amounts of
butter. (Overheating, typically in a processor, will
make the purée heavy, almost stringy.) Proportions
depend to some extent on the type of potato, but
are mainly a matter of taste. Lastly, season with salt
and white pepper (to avoid speckling).

Potatoes Sautéed, pan-fried, deep-fried

Here I concentrate on frying, a method well suited to potatoes, especially floury types. Their hard, starchy texture stands up well to high heat. The challenge is to brown the exterior in the same time as cooking the interior until tender. Here are a few points to bear in mind. First of all, the potatoes must be cut uniformly in small or thin pieces. Secondly, once cut, rinsing or soaking removes some of the starch, keeping deep-fried potatoes from sticking together and helping to crisp them. A ten-minute soak will do. Lastly, cooking temperature must be closely watched. Sautéed and pan-fried potatoes need a brisk but not scorching heat, so they cook to the centre while becoming very brown and crisp on the outside. For deep-fried wafer-thin potato crisps and matchsticks, fat should be very hot so the slivers of potato brown in a minute or so. When deep-frying larger chunks of potato, including the classic chips, potatoes are cooked twice, first at 160°C/325°F so they soften and cook through, then at 190°C/375°F so they darken to a triumphant golden crisp. Always ensure the fat is at the right temperature before adding the potatoes and never overcrowd the pan or you will cool the fat too much.

STAGES IN COOKING

▶ **UNDERCOOKED AND PALE** — scarcely browned; floppy rather than crisp; flavour fatty.

◀ **PERFECT** — golden (if deep-fried) with darker edges (if pan-fried or sautéed); crisp outside, tender, almost floury texture inside; flavour nutty with no trace of grease. Note: to keep potatoes crisp, be sure to brown them really thoroughly, especially when pan-frying.

Root vegetables including sweet potatoes

Root vegetables used to get rough treatment in the kitchen. Standard practice was to boil them to a watery, tasteless pulp, reviving all-too-vivid memories of school lunches from the steam table. Today's creative approach to roots is a constant, joyful surprise. For the cook, sweet potatoes and yams behave very like potatoes (see pages 74-76), though they belong to different botanical families. Their skin colours run the autumn gamut of golden orange to pink to brown and even violet, though the flesh is often a pastel tint. Roots are not only versatile, they are inexpensive, and require little labour apart from peeling. Even that can be avoided if you're prepared to eat the chewy, but tasty, skin. Take care to cut roots into even pieces so they all cook at the same speed, and watch out for fibres in large, old roots, particularly celery, swede and parsnip. When boiling, immerse roots in plenty of cold salted water and cook with the lid on, simmering gently so they do not break up. You'll find a touch of sugar in many recipes for roots – it's an old trick for developing their flavour.

VEGETABLE STOCK

To make about 1.5 litres/2⅓ pints of vegetable stock: in a large pan combine 3 onions, sliced, 3 carrots, thinly sliced, 3 stalks of celery, sliced, and 2 garlic cloves, lightly crushed, with about 2 litres/3¼ pints water. Add a bouquet garni and 1 generous teaspoon black peppercorns. Bring slowly to the boil, skimming often. Simmer uncovered ¾-1 hour; until the liquid is reduced by about one-quarter. Strain, let cool and store in refrigerator.

▶ **PERFECT** – tender but does not break up when pierced with point of a knife; when drained, flesh is moist not watery and slightly translucent; flavour is mellow, sometimes sweet as for carrots, or piquant as with turnip and artichoke. Note: vegetables for soup or purée should be more tender, but not so cooked as to be watery.

Onions

Onions are the foundation of so many dishes that doing without them is unimaginable. It is important not only to choose the right type for the job, but also to cook them to the right stage. Yellow onions are the most versatile. Their flavour can vary from harsh when raw, to mild and sweet when sliced and sweated gently in oil or butter and their own juices. When onions are cooked further, juices darken slowly to caramel, a rich flavouring for a quiche. Yellow varieties become pungent, the basis of the best onion soup. Do not let onions scorch, however, as they will turn unpleasantly acrid. Other types of onion have more specific uses. The first white onions of spring, mild and sweet, are wonderful glazed in butter and sugar, or simmered in chicken stock with a little honey. Full-grown white and yellow onions may be stuffed.

STAGES IN COOKING

▼ **PERFECT SOFT** – sliced or chopped onions are translucent, moist and meltingly tender with no trace of browning; whole onions are plump, juicy, tender when pierced with a skewer but still holding shape; for all types, flavour is sweet and rich.

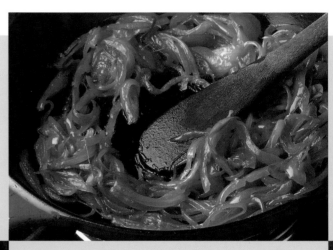

▲ **PERFECT LIGHTLY BROWNED** – sliced or chopped onions are rich golden brown, slightly crisp, with moisture evaporated; flavour is savoury and mellow.

▲ **PERFECT** – flesh can easily be squeezed in pieces from a whole bulb; whether peeled or still in skin, garlic clove or shallot bulb is tender when pinched or pierced with point of a knife; flesh is moist and very aromatic.

▼ **PERFECT VERY BROWN AND CARAMELIZED** – sliced onions have become a confit, cooked down to a dark purée with no trace of scorching; flavour is intense, mellow and sweet with caramel.

WHOLE GARLIC AND SHALLOT

For centuries, garlic and shallots have been used as flavourings, but recently they've taken centre stage in dishes like confit or roasted garlic and shallot. Twin garlic and shallot purées regularly appear on our table with roast lamb, a contrast of pungent and sweet. To temper the flavour of winter garlic (which can be harsh), discard any green sprout from the centre of the clove and blanch the garlic in boiling water for 1-2 minutes. When roasting garlic or shallots, I like to squeeze the cooked flesh from skins, then chop or purée it with herbs such as thyme or oregano and a little oil. Season the purée to taste and spread it on crusty bread. If the garlic or shallot has been cooked too long, cut away any charred portions, then chop and use the flesh to flavour other dishes.

Mushrooms

It seems to me that mushrooms can be one of the very best cultivated vegetables, comparable to the elusive wild mushrooms that I can just remember gathering in the fields as a child. Apart from the ubiquitous common mushroom, today the half-dozen so-called exotic varieties which are commonly available include cep, chanterelle, cloud ear, enokitake, chestnut, hedgehog, morel, oyster and shiitake. All can be relied upon to bring colour and meaty flavour to a dish – though at a certain price. Thanks to modern methods, almost all mushrooms now have clean caps and very little to trim off the stem – the woody stems of shiitake are an exception, as they must be trimmed level with the cap. Most mushroom caps have tender skins, though you may want to peel some chestnut mushrooms. Do remember that many varieties of mushroom produce a lot of liquid when cooked; if necessary, drain it off and/or just evaporate it off over high heat.

STAGES IN COOKING

▼ **UNDERCOOKED AND WOODY** – flesh is firm and resistant to a fork, with juices not yet developed; colour pale and flavour not yet released.

▲ **PERFECT** – texture tender and juicy, soft enough to cut with a fork; colour striking (pale cream for common mushrooms) and flavour intense.

Wild mushroom fricassee with hazelnuts

I find this earthy combination outstanding with roast game.

SERVES 4-6

125 g/4 oz chopped hazelnuts
500 g/1 pound mixed wild mushrooms
(ceps with orange and black
chanterelles is ideal), stems
trimmed
60 g/2 oz butter
2 shallots, finely chopped
1 garlic clove, finely chopped
salt and pepper
2 tablespoons chopped parsley
squeeze of lemon juice

Preheat the oven to 175°C/350°F/gas4. Spread the hazelnuts on a baking sheet, and toast in the preheated oven until lightly browned, stirring once, 12-15 minutes.

Brush then rinse the mushrooms quickly with cold water. Never soak mushrooms or they soften to pulp. Drain well. Leave small ones whole and cut large in half or quarters.

Melt half butter in a large sauté pan. Add shallots and sauté until soft but not brown, 1-2 minutes. Add mushrooms, garlic, salt and pepper and sauté briskly, tossing and stirring, for 3-5 minutes. Add remaining butter, nuts and parsley. Sauté 1-2 minutes more. Sprinkle with lemon juice and adjust seasoning.

Stir-fried vegetables

Greens, roots, stalks, sprouts – almost any vegetable blends happily in a stir-fry; the added flavourings give it its character. When making your choice of vegetable, take contrast of colour into account as well as taste. Cooking should be rapid, particularly at the start, so crisp textures and fresh flavours are maintained. Ingredients are added in order of their cooking times, so decide ahead what is old or young and how long it will take. Depending on toughness, cut each in large or small pieces, keeping them even-sized so they cook at the same speed. If at the end the vegetables are too crunchy, add a little stock or water, cover and simmer briefly until done. For more on stir-frying technique, see page 24.

STAGES IN COOKING

▼ **PERFECT** – vegetables just tender but still firm, some of them crisp; colours bright with plenty of contrast; seasoning vigorous without drowning tastes of vegetables.

▲ OVERCOOKED – vegetables limp and faded, often soggy; flavours flat.

Vietnamese stir-fried green beans with sesame

In Vietnamese restaurants, you'll see the whole family sitting around the table trimming beans for recipes like this one. The same seasoning mix is delicious with shredded cabbage and, of course, with yellow beans.

SERVES 3-4

500 g/1 pound green beans, trimmed

1 tablespoon toasted sesame seeds

1.25-cm/¹/₂ -inch piece of fresh ginger, finely chopped

1 tablespoon Chinese black beans, finely chopped

3 garlic cloves, finely chopped

2 tablespoons vegetable oil

2 tablespoons dark soy sauce, more to taste

1 tablespoon rice wine

1 teaspoon sugar

Combine the ginger, black beans and garlic in a small bowl.

Heat the wok over high heat until very hot. Drizzle in just enough vegetable oil to coat bottom and sides. Add the ginger mixture and stir-fry until just aromatic, 5-10 seconds.

Add the green beans and stir-fry over high heat until they turn a darker green and start to pop, 5-7 minutes. Stir the sauce, rice wine and sugar into the green beans and continue stir-frying until the beans look slightly blackened and withered, 3-4 minutes longer.

Take the wok from heat, add the sesame oil and toasted sesame seeds, and stir to coat beans. Taste and adjust the seasoning with soy sauce and more sesame oil if necessary.

Serve at once.

Deep-fried vegetables

To protect them from the hot fat, vegetable fritters may be simply tossed in flour after being soaked in milk or dipped in frothy egg white. Of the batter coatings, Japanese tempura is the most delicate. More substantial batters are lightened with egg, beer or yeast. A flour, egg and breadcrumb coating can be used, but is only suitable for robust vegetables like aubergine, okra and courgette. Remember that the coating also flavours the vegetables, so season it well. Even lighter than fritters are the few vegetables that can be deep-fried without a coating – thinly sliced courgette, or leek and ginger julienne. You can make chips of roots such as celeriac, beetroot and sweet potato. The potato fries so well it merits its own entry (page 76)! For more on deep-frying technique, see page 22.

STAGES IN COOKING

▼ UNDERCOOKED AND PALE – coating pallid, soggy; vegetables fatty, often chewy.

▲ **PERFECT** – coating evenly coloured a pale to deep gold; crisp and light when drained (often shape of vegetable is visible through the coating); vegetable flavour is vivid, texture soft or firm but not soggy.

Braised & glazed vegetables

When braising vegetables, I usually simmer them with wine, stock or water and flavourings such as tomato or dried fruits to develop their natural mellow flavours. They may first be browned in oil or butter to concentrate the taste. Carrots, celeriac, leek, sweet potato, turnip, onion and fennel are top choices. For glazing with oil or butter in their own juices, the same robust vegetables hold their shape well.

STAGES IN COOKING

▼ **PERFECT** – vegetable tender but does not break up when pierced with point of a knife; butter and sugar pale golden brown and colours bright; flavours robust and sweet.

▲ OVERCOOKED – vegetables soft, almost falling apart when poked with a knife; sugar starting to caramelize, flavour often bitter.

Glazed root vegetables

Common roots, such as the carrots, turnips and onions used here, are transformed by glazing.

SERVES 6-8
500 g/1 pound baby carrots, or larger carrots, peeled and cut into even pieces
500 g/1 pound baby or larger beetroots, peeled and cut into even pieces
500 g/1 pound baby onions, trimmed and peeled
60 g/2 oz butter
2 tablespoons sugar
salt and pepper
500 ml/16 fl oz water, more if needed
3-4 tablespoons chopped parsley

Put raw vegetables in separate pans large enough for each of them to form an even layer on the bottom. To each pan, add one-third of the butter and 2 teaspoons sugar, with salt and pepper to taste. Pour over just enough water to cover the vegetables halfway. Cover, bring to the boil and simmer until the vegetables are almost tender, 10-25 minutes depending on type and size.

Remove the lids and boil each pan until the liquid has evaporated to a syrupy glaze and the vegetables are done, shaking the pan occasionally to turn the vegetables and coat them evenly.

Sprinkle the vegetables with parsley and toss to mix. Adjust the seasoning. Serve each vegetable separately or mix them together, if you like – the beetroots will, however, tend to bleed slightly.

Puréed vegetables

Vegetable purées are more of a challenge than they seem. It's no good simply mashing a vegetable. First, be sure to choose one which purées easily, such as carrot or pumpkin; fibrous types like leek do not do well. The starch in dried vegetables, particularly kidney beans, is helpful in lightening and binding a purée, and some puréed vegetables such as celeriac need some potato added for starch. Be sure the vegetable is thoroughly cooked (usually boiled or steamed) so it breaks up smoothly. Long cooking means that bland vegetables like pumpkin and squash become even blander, needing plenty of seasonings. To soften and lighten them, most purées are beaten over the heat with butter and cream in generous quantities. Finally, a bright-coloured vegetable is a bonus, though the white of turnip or celeriac has its own appeal. The addition of some chopped fresh green herbs always helps a poor colour.

STAGES IN COOKING

▼ **TOO THIN** – purée watery, almost thin enough to pour; colour pale and flavour flat.

▼ **TEXTURE LUMPY OR COARSE** – consistency of purée uneven, watery at edges, often sticky on the tongue; colour may be dull.

▲ **PERFECT** – purée (here, sweet potatoes) is smooth, light and falls from spoon; holds a clear shape without being sticky; colour is clear, usually pastel; flavour fragrant.

Grilled & roasted vegetables

Given the dry heat of grilling and roasting, it is logical to choose robust vegetables, preferably with plenty of natural juice. First choice are vegetable fruits – tomatoes, sweet peppers and squash. Roots such as carrot, turnip and celeriac roast well, and green vegetables like asparagus, chicory and radicchio are good grilled, providing it is done with care. Beware of charring vegetables and overwhelming their, often mild, flavours. Constant basting is the key, though the need for basting in the oven can be reduced by covering with foil. Before cooking begins, moisten the vegetables well with oil or butter, salt, pepper and seasonings. You'll find that if left to marinate for just 5-10 minutes the vegetables will do even better. To obtain the attractive lined pattern on vegetables left by a hot grill, preheat the grill rack thoroughly, then brush it with oil before adding the vegetables. Leave them until they are well toasted with score marks before moving or turning over.

STAGES IN COOKING

▼ **PERFECT** – vegetables moist, tender but still holding shape; surface lightly browned and edges charred; flavours intense, slightly smoky, colours bright.

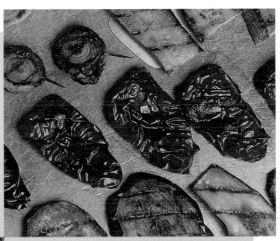

▲ OVERCOOKED AND DRY – vegetables dry and shrivelled; colours faded and flavour often harsh.

Vegetable terrines & moulds

Colourful vegetables such as carrot, green beans, broccoli, spinach and peas look best in terrines. Those with a high natural moisture content, for instance tomato or squash, are not suitable, nor are fibrous vegetables like leeks which could tear the terrine apart when sliced. Vegetable purées to be moulded in a terrine should be stiff (see Puréed vegetables, page 86). Vegetable terrines divide into two basic types: simple moulds made of vegetable purée bound with egg, and more complicated terrines with whole or chopped vegetables arranged in layers and held together with a separate mixture, often an egg custard. In both, the vegetables are lightly precooked. During precooking, the vegetables should be seasoned very well. Most importantly, maximum moisture must be extracted if the terrine is to hold its shape. When moulding a layered terrine, put the softest vegetables on the bottom, so that when unmoulded, the stiffer ones form a firm base.

STAGES IN COOKING

▼ **UNDERCOOKED** – mould soft in the centre when pressed, collapses when unmoulded.

▼ **OVERCOOKED** – mould is coarse-textured, lightly browned and tending to crumble.

▲ **PERFECT** – tall and with straight sides, the mould is light-textured when cut.

Two-colour vegetable timbale

SERVES 4 AS A STARTER OR
  8 AS A SIDE DISH
1 kg/2 lb cauliflower
2 tablespoons double
  cream
1 kg/2 lb spinach, stems
  removed
salt and white pepper
pinch of nutmeg
2 eggs

FOR THE RED PEPPER SAUCE
2 red sweet peppers
1 tablespoon butter
1 onion, chopped
2 garlic cloves, chopped
2 tomatoes, peeled, seeded
  and chopped

eight 125-ml/4-fl oz dariole
  moulds or ramekins

Preheat the oven to 175°C/350°F/gas4. Trim the cauliflower and cut it into florets, discarding the stems. Bring a pan of salted water to the boil. Add the florets and simmer, uncovered, until very tender, 8-12 minutes. Drain well. Purée with the double cream until smooth.

Pack spinach in a large heavy pan, cover and cook just until wilted, stirring occasionally, 3-4 minutes. Let cool, then squeeze out all water. Purée. Transfer purées to 2 pans. Cook over low heat, stirring constantly, until nearly all liquid has evaporated and they pull away from pan sides, 5-7 minutes. Let cool, then adjust seasoning, adding nutmeg to spinach.

Meanwhile, make sauce: preheat grill; roast peppers under grill, turning until skins char, 7-10 minutes. Put in plastic bag to steam and loosen skins. Let cool. Peel peppers, discard cores and seeds, and chop. Melt butter in a frying pan. Stir in onion and garlic and sauté until soft but not brown, 3-4 minutes. Purée in food processor with peppers, tomatoes, salt and pepper. Transfer to small pan and cook over low heat until hot and slightly thickened, 1-2 minutes. Adjust seasoning.

Butter moulds. Half-fill roasting pan with water and bring to boil on the stove. Whisk 1 egg with salt and pepper and stir into cauliflower purée. Repeat for spinach purée. Spoon some cauliflower purée into each mould, then top with some spinach puree. Place moulds in water bath and bring back to boil. Bake in oven until done, 15-20 minutes.

Reheat sauce and spoon on some warmed plates. Run a knife around the edge of the moulds, turn out on the plates and serve at once.

STAGES IN COOKING

▼ **PERFECT** – mould is just set with moist surface; mixture firm when pressed and a skewer inserted in centre is hot when withdrawn after 30 seconds; colours vivid.

▲ **OVERCOOKED** – mixture shrinks from sides of mould, with cooking juices expelled around edges; flavour is flat.

Pasta, grains & pulses

My father, british-born and traditional to the core, would never touch pasta or rice if he could avoid it – 'foreign frippery', he said. How different we are today! Pasta has become a staple, from simple spaghetti to homemade ravioli filled with luxuries like lobster and wild mushrooms. Half a dozen robust grains are routinely available, while long-ignored beans and lentils are back in style.

Oddly enough, pasta – which is no more than a plain paste of wheat flour and water, with or without eggs – is in its way more versatile than any of the grains, being shaped in dozens of different string or hollow shapes as well as being stuffed for ravioli or cannelloni, or layered with sauce as in lasagne. Pasta dishes have developed far beyond Italian classics like *tagliatelle con ragù bolognese* and *penne al pesto* to contemporary creations such as fettuccine with braised garlic and balsamic vinegar or prawn-stuffed ravioli in fragrant broth. You'll find advice on kneading and rolling your own pasta dough on page 92.

Grains offer a wide palette of tastes and plenty of chew – be sure to cook them thoroughly as when undercooked they are crunchy and indigestible. In the West, grains are invariably treated one of three ways: boiled or steamed to be light and fluffy, simmered as a pilaf, or cooked with quantities of liquid as a creamy, soft risotto. The grain may be whole, cracked or coarsely ground as a meal, when it is simmered to purées familiar as polenta and grits. When cooked to be fluffy, the flavour of a grain comes through clearly as with nutty buckwheat or fragrant white basmati rice. In pilaf and risotto the intrinsic taste of the grain blends with vegetables and spices, sometimes with the addition of fish, shellfish or meats. However, it must never be overwhelmed.

As for beans, peas and lentils, it's the choice of flavourings which gives the ethnic twist, as in Portuguese broad beans with pork, cumin and coriander, or French *salade de lentilles* with a vinaigrette dressing. These pulses are prime sources of hearty winter soups, and spicy purées, many of Asian ancestry.

We rely on grains, pasta and pulses for so many simple, everyday dishes. Given their low cost, it is well worth buying the best and seeking out a reliable, fresh supply. Grains, pasta and pulses are high in carbohydrates and turn bland and powdery when stale – debris in the bottom of the package is a bad sign. All offer excellent nutritional value. And all, even pasta, remain stubbornly, refreshingly ethnic.

VEAL AND HERB CANNELLONI, PAGE 93

Spaghetti & string pasta; macaroni & shaped pasta

There's some astonishingly good pasta around these days in the local shops, from top-quality dried spaghetti and string pasta like angel hair to reliable 'fresh' noodles (in fact, lightly dried) such as tagliatelle and linguine. Start with good raw materials and all you have to do is add character in the dressing. A few tiny pasta shapes – letters and stars for instance – are designed for soup, and the rice-shaped pasta called orzo can be served like a true grain. An Italian friend of mine adds a few comments on cooking pasta: use plenty of salted water, allowing 4 litres/7 pints of water and 1 tablespoon salt per 500 g/1 lb of pasta. A spoonful of oil will discourage the water from boiling over after the pasta is added. Once boiling, stir the pasta to separate strands, then let it simmer until done (rapid boiling can break up pieces before they're cooked).

STAGES IN COOKING

► ▼ **PERFECT** –
pasta tender but still firm to the bite (al dente); string pasta can be cut with your thumbnail.

Pieces show no tendency to stick together; flavour nutty.

► **OVERCOOKED** –
pasta swollen, limp and soft; pieces sticky, especially string pasta.

KNEADING AND ROLLING FRESH PASTA DOUGH

For egg-rich pasta dough, plain flour is best. Add a minimum of liquid – classic proportions are 100 g/3¼ oz flour to 1 large egg and a pinch of salt, with no water. It should be so firm that kneading is hard.

Lightly flour work surface and push ball of dough away from you with heel of one hand, holding it with the other. Lift dough from surface, give it a half-turn and push away from you again. Knead until it elastic and peels from surface in one piece, 5-10 minutes. Let rest, covered with bowl, for at least 30 minutes to lose elasticity. Pat dough flat into a round with rolling pin. Roll, turning and moving it so it doesn't stick, to postcard thickness.

Purists insist pasta is best hand-kneaded and rolled, but I find it much easier to use a pasta machine. Divide dough into 2-3 pieces and cover all but one with a cloth. Set machine at its widest setting and work dough through it. Fold into 2 or 3 and continue working through the machine until satin-smooth and elastic, 8-10 minutes, dusting with flour if sticky. Pasta dough should always be firm, so don't hesitate to work in extra flour during kneading.

When dough is very smooth, start reducing machine settings until dough is a 15-cm/6-inch strip the thickness of a postcard, the thinnest setting.

Cannelloni, lasagne & layered pasta

You can buy dried or fresh commercial pasta, or make your own fresh pasta sheets (see left). I've had good luck with commercial pasta, particularly given the complex sauces and stuffings used with layered pasta, but I have to admit that cannelloni or lasagne with homemade dough are incomparable. Before layering or stuffing, the pasta must, of course, be boiled and drained on paper towels. Simmer the sheets or tubes in plenty of salted water so they don't stick together and undercook them slightly as they will cook further with the filling. To make filling cannelloni tubes easy, use a pastry bag, leaving the tip open without a tube. For cannelloni, cut flat sheets in rectangles and roll them around your filling.

▲ **PERFECT** – pasta just tender when cut with knife; filling is rich, moist and hot; flavour hearty and colours contrasting and bright.

Veal and herb cannelloni

Cannelloni means 'big pipes' in Italian, reflecting their tubular shape.

SERVES 4

375 g/³/₄ pound minced veal
8 dried cannelloni (about 150 g/5 oz)
60 g/2 oz chopped mixed herbs, such as sage, thyme, parsley
60 g/2 oz grated Parmesan cheese
1 egg
125 ml/4 fl oz milk

pastry bag without tube

FOR THE BÉCHAMEL SAUCE

500 ml/16 fl oz milk, more if needed
1 large slice of onion
1 bay leaf
¹/₂ teaspoon black peppercorns
45 g/1¹/₂ oz butter
20 g/³/₄ oz flour
salt and white pepper
generous pinch of nutmeg

Preheat oven to 175°C/350°F/gas4. Butter a medium baking dish. Bring a large pot of salted water to the boil.

Make sauce: scald milk with onion, bay leaf and peppercorns. Cover and leave to infuse off heat, 10-15 minutes. In a heavy-based pan, melt butter; whisk in flour and cook, stirring, until foaming but not browned, about 1 minute. Off heat, strain in hot milk. Whisk well and bring to boil, whisking constantly until sauce thickens. Season with salt, pepper and nutmeg, and simmer for 1-2 minutes. Take off heat, cover and let cool.

Add cannelloni to boiling water and simmer until done, 8-10 minutes or as instructions. Using slotted spoon, transfer to a bowl of cold water to cool, then drain thoroughly.

Stir together veal, half the sauce, herbs and half cheese. Season well. Beat in egg. Pipe into cannelloni and set in baking dish. Whisk milk into remaining sauce and bring just to the boil. It should lightly coat spoon – if not, thin with more milk. Adjust seasoning. Spoon over cannelloni to coat. Sprinkle with remaining cheese. Bake until done, 40-50 minutes.

Ravioli & stuffed pasta

Here I'm looking at delectable homemade packages – ravioli, tortellini and their cousins – once the province of Italian grandmothers but now international fare. We begin by making an egg-enriched pasta dough as described on page 92, then kneading it and rolling it through a pasta machine until satin-smooth and elastic. At the end, you'll have long ribbons of dough, ready to shape at once into packages. Shaping the packages is a matter of patience, as they must be cut and sealed with care. Be sure the filling is assertive to offset the neutral dough, and don't be tempted to add too much — my usual failing — or the package will burst. Ravioli and pasta packages are best cooked in plenty of water at a brisk simmer to keep the pasta moving so it does not stick together. For fragile packages, steaming can be safer — but don't overlap them as they cook.

STAGES IN COOKING

▼ **PERFECT** – parcels (here, ravioli) clearly shaped, with filling tightly sealed; when cut with a thumbnail or knife, pasta feels tender with no hard core; when tasted, pasta is tender but still firm to the bite (al dente); flavour is hearty and fresh.

▲ OVERCOOKED – parcels swollen and often leaking; pasta is limp and sticky; texture soft and flavour pasty.

Fluffy whole & cracked grains

For fluffy grains, water – and lots of it – is the usual cooking medium. The grains may be boiled, simmered or steamed, and the key to lightness is to limit the effects of dissolved starch. Much depends on the type of grain and whether it is whole or cracked. Clearly, whole grains give off much less starch than when they are cracked and their structure is cut open. Thorough rinsing of the grain with cold water before cooking launches the process and cleans the grains as well. When boiling, allow generous quantities of water – at least four times the volume of the grain – and boil rapidly to keep the grains bubbling and separate. When steaming, spread the grain in a shallow layer so moisture is absorbed and penetrates evenly. Grains form a delicious, nutty background for all sorts of dishes and seasonings.

STAGES IN COOKING

UNDERCOOKED ▼
– grains (here boiled white rice) separate but densely packed with hard, starchy core.

▼ OVERCOOKED – grains soft, often burst and falling into mush when stirred; when tasted, grains pulpy offering no resistance; flavour mealy, colour dull.

▲ PERFECT – boiled grains fluffy and separate; large grains can be cut with thumbnail; tender but still firm to the bite when tasted; flavour earthy, colour clear.

Risottos

For risotto, the grain (almost always short-grain rice, arborio being the most famous variety) is simmered quite rapidly. It is essential to stir constantly for the 25 minutes or so of cooking. As with pilaf, rice for risotto is toasted first in butter or oil (or a combination of the two). This process encourages the grains to separate, yet still allows them to release starch and make the risotto creamy. The longer you toast the rice, the longer it will take to cook to its creamy finale. Some wine, usually white, is added for flavour and stirred until evaporated. Then boiling liquid, typically a light stock, is ladled in little by little so the temperature of the rice does not drop. Constant stirring helps keep the rice moving as it cooks; in time, the rice will soften and thicken the liquid to a creamy consistency, absorbing 4-5 times its own volume. In Venice a risotto is served *al onda*, soft enough to pour, but elsewhere in Italy it's preferred al dente, somewhat firmer to the bite. Either way, risotto should be creamy without being soupy or dry, and never mushy.

STAGES IN COOKING

▼ **PERFECT SOFT** – grain falls easily from spoon, with liquid thickened to a creamy consistency; flavour mellow and colour clear.

▲ **PERFECT FIRM** – grain lightly thickened, just holds a shape with no trace of stickiness; flavour earthy.

Grain pilafs

When cooking by the pilaf method, grains are fried in hot fat before being simmered until a measured amount of liquid has been absorbed. Be sure to brown the grains thoroughly first in order to seal the surface as this helps to keep them separate. In one recipe for cooking whole kasha (roasted buckwheat groats), the grains are first cooked with a whole egg, stirring constantly over high heat to separate them and to encourage lightness. One and a half to twice the volume of liquid to grain is usual. Less liquid means drier, fluffier grains, but some tough varieties such as wild rice and barley need more time and a larger amount of liquid to cook completely. When a pilaf is cooked, the grains should have absorbed all the liquid, but taste to make sure they also are tender. Leave the pilaf to cool for at least 10 minutes so the grains contract slightly, then stir gently with a fork to separate them without crushing.

STAGES IN COOKING

▼ **PERFECT** – whole grain pilaf (here, brown rice pilaf) grains separate, liquid absorbed so rest is lightly thickened and creamy; when tasted, grains are soft but still resistant; flavour full-bodied and rich.

▲ **PERFECT** – cracked grain pilaf (here, bulghur) grains separate when stirred with fork; texture fluffy and light, slightly chewy; flavour full-bodied, colour clear.

Polenta & ground grains

Coarsely ground grains are also called meals, the most common example being the cornmeal used to make polenta and the quick breads and savoury puddings so popular in the southern USA. The crunchy bite and vigorous taste of stoneground cornmeal is startlingly different from bland commercial types, well worth a search of your market shelves. Other meals include buckwheat grits, hominy grits and spelt. Semolina, made from wheat, and tapioca, made from dried yuca root, also behave like meals. Ground grains are usually cooked by whisking a steady stream of grain into simmering water or milk. Use a heavy pan which sits firmly on the stove so one hand is free to trickle in the grain while you whisk or stir with the other. Cooking time depends mainly on the coarseness of the meal. Seasoning is important – be generous to avoid an effect of nursery pap. Ground grains are often served like rice as a background for savoury stews. Polenta, for instance, may come as a soft purée, falling easily from the spoon, or it may be left to set and then grilled or fried in cakes.

STAGES IN COOKING

▼ **PERFECT** – mixture (here, polenta) is smooth, thick but not sticky and falls easily from spoon; flavour is full-bodied, colour clear.

▲ **OVERCOOKED** – texture dense and sticky, clinging to spoon; flavour dull.

Dried beans, peas & lentils

Beans and whole peas have thick skins, so need soaking for several hours in cold water. To speed the process, you can pour boiling water over them and leave for half an hour. Don't add salt or any acid, such as vinegar or tomato, until cooking is well advanced as the skins will toughen for good. Tap water high in minerals can toughen skins, so use filtered water. Some pulses contain toxins, easily dissolved during cooking. To be sure, boil beans rapidly for at least 10 minutes. Lentils and split peas need only to be brought to the boil.

STAGES IN **COOKING**

▶ **PERFECT** – beans, peas or lentils soft and tender; for beans or peas, a few skins starting to burst; most liquid absorbed, so rest is lightly thickened; colour clear not muddy; flavour mellow.

◀ **UNDERCOOKED AND TOUGH** – texture chewy, especially skins on beans or peas; juices watery; flavour not yet developed.

DRIED BEAN, PEA AND LENTIL PURÉES

Dried beans, peas and lentils are a fertile source of earthy soups and full-flavoured purées, since they fall easily into a mush when thoroughly cooked. Long simmering will not spoil their flavour (how different from fresh vegetables!). In fact, the key is to cook the beans or peas so long they start to fall apart. By this stage most of the water should have been absorbed; split peas or lentils will now be ready for puréeing in a food processor or with an immersion blender until smooth. However, the skin of beans and whole peas spoils the creamy texture of a perfect purée or soup, so they should be worked through a sieve. By all means, if you like a coarse-textured soup, simply crush the beans or peas to a chunky paste. For tips on vegetable purées, see Vegetables.

▲ **PERFECT FOR PURÉES** – very soft and falls from the spoon with no trace of stickiness; purée has texture but is smooth on the tongue; flavour is full-bodied and fragrant.

Eggs

Remember one simple fact about cooking eggs – they coagulate rapidly at relatively low temperatures, 63°C/145°F for whites and 66°C/150°F for yolks. This is why it is so important to cook them at moderate, rather than high, temperatures. If you look at the various cooking methods, eggs are invariably shielded from direct heat, either by the shell, by a heavy dish or pan, or by cooking in water or a water bath. The high heat needed for a folded omelette is an exception, but even then a thick pan is mandatory.

The egg itself provides a variety of shapes and textures, not to mention eye-catching colour. Its flavour is an ideal background for other more robust ingredients, like bacon, spinach, truffles or cheese – in small quantities of course. Whatever the flavouring, a careful hand is needed, for it's all too easy to overwhelm the delicate aroma of a freshly laid egg with chilli or soy sauce, even with too much salt and pepper. It is hard to beat simple dishes like scrambled eggs with fresh herbs, or a baked egg seasoned with salt and pepper and topped with a spoonful of cream.

We are all warned not to eat too many eggs and, as it happens, a proper serving is difficult to gauge. While a single soft-boiled egg is surprisingly satisfying, a two-egg omelette or portion of scrambled eggs can seem sadly deficient. On the other hand, a more modest serving of one poached or baked egg does well as a first course, providing a generous garnish is included.

Remember that cooked eggs cannot sit for long. A soufflé is the classic example of a dish we must wait for, rather than it wait for us. Omelettes, baked and fried eggs, even a lightly boiled egg, are all the better for serving promptly. Then their simple freshness can be appreciated to the full.

HARD-BOILED EGGS WITH GARLIC AND HERB TOPPING, PAGE 103

Boiled eggs

You'd think boiling eggs would be easy, but there are snares even to this simple process. Very fresh eggs take a minute or two longer to cook, as do extra-large ones. Shells crack easily during cooking, particularly those from battery hens, so start cooking in cold water so the egg heats slowly, and time from the moment the water comes to the boil: 3-4 minutes for a soft-boiled egg, 5-7 minutes for mollet (below) and 10-12 minutes for hard-boiled. Boiling is a misnomer as eggs should be simmered, both to keep the shells intact and so as not to toughen the whites. To seal any white which may leak, add a spoonful of vinegar or salt to the water. As an egg ages, an air pocket forms at the end of the shell and its expansion when heated often causes the shell to crack, so some cooks prick the flat end of the egg to let air escape. Remember that eggs continue to cook from residual heat unless cooled quickly in lots of cold water.

STAGES IN COOKING

▼ **PERFECT MOLLET** – yolk is soft but not runny and vivid in colour, white is set; shell can be peeled with care. Often served in a sauce or aspic, like a poached egg.

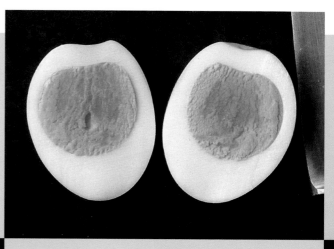

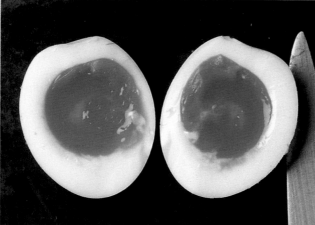

▲ **PERFECT HARD-BOILED CENTRE** – both yolk and white are firmly set; yolk is slightly pale in colour; shell is easy to peel. Used for slicing, stuffing and serving hot in sauce or cold with mayonnaise.

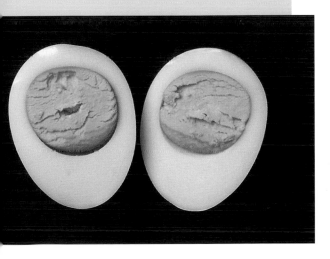

Hard-boiled eggs with garlic and herb topping

Serve a tomato and fresh basil salad with this simple little recipe from the Italian island of Sardinia.

SERVES 6

6 eggs
salt
4 tablespoons olive oil
4 teaspoons red wine vinegar

1 garlic clove, finely chopped
3 tablespoons dry breadcrumbs
2 teaspoons finely chopped parsley

Put the eggs in a medium pan, generously cover with cold water and add 2 teaspoons salt to help seal any egg white which may start to leak from the shells. Bring to the boil and simmer until hard-boiled, 10-12 minutes. Cool the eggs in cold water. Peel, rinse them under cold running water and dry them. Slice each egg in half lengthwise.

Heat the oil, vinegar and a large pinch of salt in a frying pan. Add the egg halves, cut side down, and cook over low heat until the vinegar has evaporated, 3-5 minutes. Turn the eggs once or twice during cooking. With a slotted spoon, transfer the eggs to a warmed platter, arranging them cut sides up, and keep warm.

Add the garlic to the frying pan and sauté over low heat until soft, about 1 minute. Stir in the breadcrumbs and cook until golden, 1-2 minutes. Spoon the mixture over the eggs. Sprinkle with the parsley and serve warm.

Poached eggs

Success in poaching depends almost entirely on the freshness of the eggs. Really fresh eggs work best, as the white is less likely to break away from the yolk once the egg is added to the boiling water. Adding 3 tablespoons of vinegar to each 1 litre/1⅔ pints of water helps prevent this from happening. Always drop each egg (four is the usual maximum) into a briskly bubbling patch of boiling water so the egg white is swirled around the yolk. Then lower the heat until the water scarcely bubbles, so the eggs cook gently without breaking. This is what poaching means. Of course, you can also poach an egg in one of those special moulds, but that's cheating. The egg loses its natural freeform shape, and is baked (or coddled, to use the nice old-fashioned term) rather than poached directly in contact with the water. A stringy or shapeless poached egg usually will taste just as good and can always be trimmed and/or swathed in a white or hollandaise sauce to disguise it.

STAGES IN **COOKING**

▼ **PERFECT** – yolk is still soft when gently prodded with fingertip; white is lightly set and clings to yolk; skin around yolk is opaque, with soft yolk inside.

▲ **WHITE FORMS STRINGS** – white no longer clings to yolk and may almost separate from it.

Fried eggs

The flavour of fat, be it butter, olive oil or lard, comes through loud and clear when frying an egg. Allow about 1 tablespoon per egg, so you can baste and cook the upper surface with hot fat, and use a heavy pan to discourage scorching. Most eggs are fried on one side only, or 'sunny side up', but they can also be flipped 'over easy' to brown the other side. For a low-fat alternative, eggs can be cooked with a minimum of fat in a non-stick pan, but the result is more like a baked than a fried egg. To keep the egg a nice shape in the pan, it often helps to break the egg first into a cup, saucer or small bowl and then slip it into the hot pan from there. The fat should be moderately hot – too cool and the egg will not cook properly, toughening as it does; too hot and it will bubble round the edges and scorch quickly.

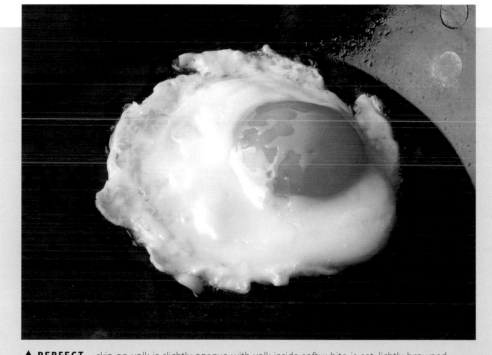

▲ **PERFECT** – skin on yolk is slightly opaque with yolk inside soft; white is set, lightly browned underneath, and clings to form a ring around the yolk.

EGGS

Rolled omelette

The key to the perfect omelette is the perfect pan. Every cook has their favourite. Personally, I go for the classic French cast-steel omelette pan, with gently sloping sides and a handle at just the right angle to make turning out easy. Before use, the pan must be 'seasoned' – baked with a layer of salt and oil so it does not stick. To clean the pan after use, simply wipe it out with a damp paper towel; never wash it. A non-stick pan is another option, though I find it doesn't brown the eggs so well.

For good flavour, be sure to brown the surface by cooking the omelette over high heat so the outside browns while the inside remains soft; with fillings that stick, such as grated cheese, fish or vegetable mixtures, begin cooking the eggs in the pan before adding the filling; use the right size pan – too few eggs in a large pan will thicken fast and toughen, while too many in a small pan will cook slowly rather like scrambled eggs.

STAGES IN COOKING

PALE AND UNDERCOOKED ▼ – surface of omelette not browned, so toasted flavour lacking.

▼ PERFECT FIRM – surface of omelette is evenly browned with no trace of scorching at any point; eggs are completely set throughout, with a firm but fluffy texture.

▲ PERFECT SOFT CENTRE – surface of omelette is lightly browned with tender texture, and centre of omelette is still slightly runny when folded over with a fork.

Flat omelette

Unlike a rolled omelette, where eggs are the leading ingredient, in a flat omelette the eggs are there to bind the filling, for example the Spanish tortilla and Italian frittata Try to use colourful ingredients that add robust texture as well as flavour. Most flat omelettes are browned on both sides to a firm cake, which can be cut into wedges for serving. Exceptions include English omelette Arnold Bennett, filled with smoked haddock then topped with Parmesan and browned under the grill. All these omelettes are cooked quite quickly, but Italian frittata is different, cooked over the lowest possible heat so the eggs puff in the pan rather like a soufflé. No matter what the nationality or style, however, what you're looking for in the perfect flat omelette remains the same.

SOUFFLÉ OMELETTES

Soufflé omelettes are light, and light-hearted. Savoury ones are made by beating the eggs for 5 minutes or more until mousse-like and thick enough to hold a light ribbon trail. The omelette may be flat or folded, and fillings are usually simple, some herbs or a little grated cheese so the eggs keep their lightness. For sweet omelettes, the eggs are separated, the whites are beaten with a little sugar to make a light meringue and then folded back into the yolks. A sweet omelette may be cooked completely on the hob, using low heat – it will take up to 10 minutes – or first browned on the underside and then quickly baked in the oven. Either way, a filling of warm fruit jam is customary, then the omelette is folded, dusted with icing sugar and hurried to the table like a true soufflé (see page 110). Both savoury and sweet soufflé omelettes should remain slightly soft in the centre.

▲ **PERFECT** – firmly set, often glossy on top and brown on underside before being flipped over; when done, evenly browned on both sides; filling is generous, so egg acts as binder; flavour is robust, often with some crunchy or chewy texture. Note: if omelette is not holding firmly enough to flip, brown under the grill.

Scrambled eggs

The best scrambled eggs are smooth, creamy and lightly thickened or firm, depending on your taste. Some cooks like to control temperature by using a double boiler or water bath when scrambling eggs, but this really isn't necessary. I simply use a heavy pan over very low heat, stirring constantly with a wooden spoon and allowing at least 3 minutes to thicken 4 or more eggs. Don't be tempted to hurry the process, though there's no need to go to the lengths of purists who heat the eggs so slowly they take half an hour to thicken. No wonder chefs competing for the highest honour in French cuisine – that of *meilleur ouvrier de France* – are often put to the test with scrambled eggs! Should your eggs overcook and separate, you can partially recover them by whisking a fresh raw egg until very smooth and stirring it into the eggs off the heat.

STAGES IN COOKING

PERFECT SOFT ▼
– eggs are creamy in texture and leave a trail when stirred; soft enough to pour, smooth and with light curds; colour varies with the egg yolks, so use deep orange yolks when you can.

▼ STIFF AND SEPARATED – curds are lumpy not smooth, often watery around edges.

▲ PERFECT FIRM – eggs just hold a shape when stirred, with soft smooth curds; for best flavour, use very fresh eggs. Note: keep stirring scrambled eggs after taking them from the heat so they do not coagulate around sides of the pan.

Baked eggs

Baked eggs come in one of two ways: en cocotte in deep ramekins for one or two eggs, or au plat in a shallow baking dish, looking more like fried eggs. Often the eggs are seasoned simply with salt and pepper – always sprinkled on the bottom of the dish to avoid spotting the surface of the egg – and topped with a spoonful of cream. You can add interest with a garnish spread in the dish, or spooned on top or around the eggs after baking. For a handy supper dish, I sometimes take leftover rice pilaf or risotto, or chopped cooked vegetables, and spread them in an oiled baking dish. I scoop hollows, drop in eggs and bake in a 175°C/350°F/gas4 oven until the eggs are set.

STAGES IN COOKING

▼ **PERFECT** – egg has a shiny 'mirror' surface, with yolk lightly thickened, white just set; surface opaque, not transparent.

▲ **HARD AND OVERCOOKED** – yolk is firm, white is dry and starting to crack on the surface – more common when egg is baked in a flat dish rather than ramekins.

Soufflé

A soufflé consists of a flavoured base puffed in the oven by whipped egg whites; here are a few signposts to success. The taller the dish, the higher the soufflé will rise, but the more likely it is to spill over – hedge your bets with a shallower dish. Brush it generously with melted butter, especially at the rim (otherwise it may stick as it rises), then freeze and coat again. Much depends on correctly beating the egg whites (see page 159) and on the consistency of the basic mixture. If this is too heavy or sticky, the egg whites cannot lighten it; if too thin, it will be difficult to fold in the egg whites. Vivid flavouring is important so that the basic mixture balances the inherent blandness of egg white.

It is essential to fold the egg whites into the basic mixture as gently as possible. It helps if you warm the mixture and stir about a quarter of the whites into it so they cook and lighten it. Then fold this carefully into the remaining

STAGES IN COOKING

▼ **PERFECT SOFT** – soufflé (here, with cheese) browned and risen high, but top still slightly concave; mixture wobbles when dish lightly shaken; centre is runny; texture smooth and light, flavour delicate and aromatic.

▲ **PERFECT WELL-COOKED** – soufflé browned and risen high with flat top; mixture is firm when dish is lightly shaken; inside, mixture is cooked through and just firm in the centre; texture is light and flavour definite.

egg whites – a metal spoon is my preferred tool for folding, though many chefs use a wooden spoon or rubber spatula. If the mixture seems to soften and lose air towards the end of folding, stop at once. A few bits of unmixed egg white are better than a flat soufflé. Set the soufflé in the bottom third of the oven on a preheated baking sheet so it gets a boost of bottom heat. Shield it from any convection fan and turn the dish during cooking so the mixture rises evenly. Note: a well-made soufflé will rise in almost any heat – the hotter the oven, the more quickly it bakes.

You may prefer a soufflé to be soft, so it forms a sauce for the firm sides. This is ideal for cheese and sweet soufflés and calls for baking at a relatively high heat, while heavier fish and vegetable soufflés are best done at a slightly lower temperature until firm throughout. In any case, guests must wait for the soufflé, never the contrary; you can keep it warm in the oven with the door open for 2-3 minutes, but no more. If a soufflé is just starting to fall, you can even reheat it for 1-2 minutes in the oven so it puffs again.

▼ **OVERBAKED** – soufflé loses height and shrivels; inside texture is uneven and tough.

▲ **ROSE UNEVENLY** – one side of soufflé flat, often sticking to rim; other side rises and may spill over.

Sauces

It's no accident that in a professional kitchen the sauce chef is at the top of the hierarchy. A sauce demands a skilled hand to balance taste and consistency just right – a mastery needed as much for contemporary butter sauces and salsas as for the grand classics like hollandaise and espagnole. This is also true at home – remember how grandmother was judged by her gravy? So important are basic sauces, such as white, velouté, brown, hollandaise, white butter and mayonnaise, that they are called 'mother sauces' with whole families of sauces descended from them.

Today we're fortunate to enjoy a much broader range of sauces than even a generation ago. Steak, for instance, may appear with a traditional Madeira or truffled brown sauce, with béarnaise, with a reduction sauce mounted with butter in the pan, with a gravy thickened with roasted garlic, or with a crispy salsa heightened with chilli and coriander. Duck may be paired with green peppercorns in place of orange, turkey with a spiced chocolate mole instead of cranberries, and sea bass with a tapenade of green olives instead of a white wine velouté.

When making a sauce, remember that it cannot exert its magic in limbo. By definition, its purpose is to complement and highlight the food which it accompanies. When tasting, don't judge a sauce on its own, like soup, but if possible pair it with the food it accompanies. This is particularly important for salad greens, which often lack intrinsic flavour. Consistency is also important. Do you want a sauce to be as thin as unthickened gravy, or lightly coat food, or mask it, or be thick enough to bind ingredients together? Judging the consistency of a sauce just right can make all the difference to a dish.

Lastly, consider the impact of a sauce. Whether delicate like egg custard, tart with a red fruit, or dark and pungent with a reduction of red wine, a sauce should have the same intensity as its companion ingredient.

PORK FILLET WITH MUSCAT WINE AND DRIED CRANBERRIES, PAGE 121

White sauce

Where would we be without white sauce? If we followed the exhortations of some contemporary chefs to leave it behind, so many familiar dishes simply would not exist. We'd have no macaroni cheese, no moussaka or creamed spinach, we'd lose half our cannelloni and lasagne, and soufflés would scarcely rate a mention. White sauce is the basis of half a dozen key creations, such as cream, mushroom, onion and oyster sauces, not to mention the French herb-and-nutmeg-scented béchamel, and mornay or cheese sauce (page 116), most important of them all. Vigorous whisking is the key to smooth consistency and a glossy finish.

STAGES IN PREPARATION

▼ **PERFECT THIN —** shiny, very pale cream colour; lightly coats back of spoon but runs off quickly; flavour is light but not bland.

▼ **PERFECT THICK —** glossy, unctuous and a rich cream colour; thick enough to bind a mixture but still falls easily from spoon; flavour is rich and full-bodied.

▲ **PERFECT MEDIUM —** generously coats back of spoon but still flows easily; smooth and glossy; flavour is creamy and fragrant.

▲ PERFECT BINDING —
smooth and stiff enough to hold mark of spoon; flavour robust, with no trace of uncooked flour.

SAUCES FOR COURSES

Thin white sauces are often used as the basis of a soup.

Medium white sauces are used for lightly coating eggs, fish, poultry, white meats and vegetables, and for some baked pasta dishes, such as cannelloni (right) or lasagne.

Thick white sauces act as a base for soufflés, stuffings and croquettes, and are better suited in baked dishes like macaroni cheese and moussaka, where a thicker consistency is needed.

Binding white sauces are, of course, used to bind ingredients together, as in choux pastry, fritters and quenelles.

For 250ml / 8fl oz you'll need:

Thin 15g / ½ oz butter and
1 tablespoon flour
Medium 20g / ¾ oz butter and
1 1/2 tablespoons flour
Thick 30g / 1 oz butter and
2 tablespoons flour
Binding 45g / 1 ½ oz butter and
3 tablespoons flour

Cheese sauce

Cheese sauce shares the claim of white sauce to being the most useful of all sauces, and personally I think it has the edge. White sauce can be bland, but cheese sauce can never be, provided it is properly seasoned. Just think of a cheese sauce – delicately golden, rich but not sticky – with fillets of sole, with sea scallops, with cauliflower, as a filling and topping for crêpes, moistening pasta or browned on top of a vegetable gratin. Cheese sauce is as easy to make as white sauce, but remember this – always whisk in the cheese off the heat and do not reheat the sauce, as it may separate and the cheese cook into strings. If your sauce ends up being too thin even after the cheese is added, whisk in 1 or 2 egg yolks and heat very gently, whisking until the sauce thickens.

STAGES IN COOKING

▼ **PERFECT** – sauce has a deep cream colour, surface is glossy, and sauce generously coats the back of spoon; flavour is lively. Note: use when a cheese sauce of thick and binding consistency is required, as in seafood and vegetable gratins, and macaroni cheese.

▲ **STRINGS IN SAUCE** – sauce is thick and long strings form when whisk is lifted.
Why: sauce was boiled, reheated or kept warm too long, so protein in cheese coagulated.
Note: this is less likely to happen with hard aged cheese such as Parmesan.

Cauliflower and Bacon Gratin

Adding broccoli and bacon to familiar cauliflower cheese makes a one-dish meal for family supper.

SERVES 4

1 medium cauliflower (about
   1.4 kg/3 pounds)
salt and pepper

FOR THE CHEESE SAUCE
600 ml/1 pint milk
1 bay leaf
1 celery leaf
1 teaspoon black
   peppercorns
pinch of freshly grated
   nutmeg

60 g/2 oz butter, more for
   the dish
30 g/1 oz flour
1 teaspoon dry mustard
175 g/6 oz Gruyère or dry
   Cheddar cheese, grated
6 slices of bacon, diced and
   dry-fried until crisp

22x33-cm/ 9x13-inch baking
   dish

Bring a large pan of salted water to the boil. Cut the cauliflower into florets, discarding the stems. Add the florets to the boiling water and, when the water comes back to the boil, cook them for 3 minutes, until they are just tender when pierced with a knife. Drain, rinse them in cold water, and drain them again thoroughly.

Preheat the oven to 200°C/400°F/gas6. Butter the baking dish.

Make the cheese sauce: in a small saucepan, bring the milk to the boil with the bay leaf, celery leaf, peppercorns and nutmeg. Cover and leave over low heat to infuse for 10 minutes. In another saucepan, melt the butter, whisk in the flour and cook, stirring, until the flour is foaming but not browned, about 1 minute. Off the heat, strain in the hot milk. Whisk well, then return to the heat and bring the sauce to a boil, whisking constantly until it thickens. Simmer it for 1-2 minutes to cook the flour thoroughly, then take it from the heat. Set aside three tablespoons of the cheese and stir the rest into the hot sauce together with the mustard, salt and pepper. Stir in the bacon. Taste and adjust seasoning.

Arrange the cauliflower florets evenly, and sprinkle with the reserved cheese. Bake in the oven until bubbling and beginning to brown, 25-30 minutes. Serve hot.

THICKENING AGENTS FOR SAUCES

Thickeners for sauces can be divided into two groups: those which are part of the sauce from the beginning, and those added at the end of cooking.

- A roux of flour and butter provides a stable robust base for white velouté and brown sauces. For brown sauces the roux should be well browned to add flavour before liquid is added.
- Beurre manié or kneaded butter is a version of a roux made by working butter and flour together, for addition in small pieces at the end.
- Fruit and vegetable purées also add a full-bodied flavour, and those of colourful vegetables like carrots and fruits like berries can improve colour.
- Egg yolks, sometimes whole eggs, are used to emulsify and lightly thicken sauces (see page 127).
- Egg yolks and cream, or simply egg yolks may be added at the end of cooking to white sauces and soups to enrich and thicken them slightly. To avoid curdling it is advisable to add some of the hot sauce to the egg and cream mixture off the heat and then stir this back into the sauce and reheat until it thickens, without boiling.
- Cornflour, potato starch and arrowroot are invaluable for last-minute thickening. They should be mixed to a thin paste with cold liquid before being added to the sauce, stirring constantly. On average, 1 teaspoon will thicken 250 ml/8 fl oz liquid. Starch thickening does not hold up well, so if you leave the sauce over heat, or reheat it, it may slacken and you'll have to add more.
- Breadcrumbs, fresh or dried, may added at any point. Used in moderation, the effect is surprisingly light, though never very smooth. A breadcrumb-thickened sauce will thicken perceptibly on standing or being reheated.
- Blood, usually pigs' blood, is a traditional thickener for dark wine sauces, particularly of game. It is whisked into the hot sauce just before serving and mustn't be boiled, or it will curdle.

Velouté sauce

Velouté sauce is made with stock or the liquid from poaching veal, poultry or fish and is usually served with its parent ingredient. This mundane definition gives little clue to the richness of a good velouté, so French chefs herald it with titles like *suprême* (chicken velouté with lemon and mushrooms) or *à la reine* (chicken breast in velouté sauce).

Velouté is outstanding with fish, often enhanced with white wine in classics such as *sauce normande* with mussels, mushrooms and prawns, or *sauce cardinale* with lobster butter. Velouté can also stand alone, flavoured with capers or tomato (*aurore*), or with lemon juice and parsley (*poulette*).

Making stocks

Stocks made from fish, chicken, veal or beef bones and vegetables, simmered with seasonings to extract maximum flavour, form the basis of many sauces and soups. Good stock is full-flavoured, fresh for fish stock, and more mellow for chicken and meat. All should be rich with gelatine, from the bones. Colour varies from almost clear for fish, to light golden for chicken to a warm golden for brown veal and beef stock, given by thorough browning of the bones and vegetables. The bones must first be blanched by bringing them to the boil and draining before they are simmered to make the stock. To intensify flavour, simmer stock until it is reduced and concentrated – if boiled further, stock eventually becomes a glaze (see page 120). For this reason, you'll see that I do not add salt to stock as it can so easily become salty when reduced.

▲ **PERFECT** – sauce lightly coats back of spoon but runs off quickly; colour a rich cream, glossy, with no tinge of grey; sauce has full-bodied flavour of stock – veal, chicken or fish – used to make it.

◄ **PERFECT** – stock clear; colour bright, pale for fish and vegetable, light golden for chicken and veal, darker for beef.

► **CLOUDY** – appearance muddy, colour often dark; flavour cloying.

Brown veal and beef stock

Veal stock is made with veal bones only, whereas beef stock has half veal bones (for gelatine) and half beef (for flavour). Vegetables suggested here are just a start and you can add many others including leeks, carrot tops, tomatoes for colour and herbs for taste; never add roots as they disintegrate. Bones and vegetables for brown stock must be well browned and this is easiest in the oven – the onion skins also add colour. At least 4 hours' simmering (and preferably 5-6) is needed to extract full flavour from the bones.

MAKES ABOUT 2.5 LITRES/4½ PINTS

- 2.5 kg/5 pounds veal (or half beef, half veal) bones, cracked in large pieces
- 2 unpeeled onions, quartered
- 2 carrots, quartered
- 1 stalk of celery, cut into pieces
- bouquet garni
- 1 teaspoon peppercorns
- 1 tablespoon tomato purée
- 3-4 garlic cloves, unpeeled (optional)
- 5 litres/9 pints water, more if needed

Preheat the oven to 260°C/500°F/gas10 or its highest setting. Put the bones in a roasting pan and roast until well browned, 30-40 minutes. Stir, add the onions, carrots and celery and continue roasting until the bones and vegetables are very brown, almost charred around the edges, 30 minutes more.

Transfer to a stockpot and add the bouquet garni, peppercorns, tomato purée, garlic if using and enough water to cover. Bring slowly to the boil, skimming often. Simmer very gently, skimming occasionally, 5-6 hours, adding more water if needed to cover. Strain and, if flavour is not concentrated, boil it until well reduced. Chill and skim off fat before using.

Stock can be kept for up to 3 days in the refrigerator, or it can be frozen. I often boil it down, freeze it in ice cube trays and store the cubes to use in small quantities.

CHICKEN STOCK

Chicken stock is made by the same general method as on the left, but substitute 1.4 kg/3 pounds raw chicken backs, necks and bones for the veal bones and do not brown them. Simmer with 1 quartered onion, 1 quartered carrot, a stalk of celery, cut into pieces, a bouquet garni, 1 teaspoon peppercorns and 4 litres/7 pints of water, allowing 2-3 hours to extract full flavour. Skim often and add more water if necessary to keep the bones covered. You can also substitute a whole chicken for the bones (use the cooked meat for another dish such as a salad) or cooked chicken carcasses, for a milder flavour. This makes about 1.5 litres/2¾ pints.

FISH STOCK

Fish stock is the only type of stock which is boiled rapidly for a short time to extract maximum flavour from the bones while still retaining a fresh taste. If the bones are not carefully washed or boiled too long, fish stock can be bitter. To make about 1 litre/1⅔ pints, boil 750 g/1½ pounds thoroughly washed fish bones and heads, cut into pieces, with 1 onion, sliced, and a bouquet garni, 1 teaspoon peppercorns, 250 ml/8 fl oz dry white wine or 4 tablespoons white wine vinegar and water just to cover. Bring to the boil, skimming often, and simmer rapidly for 20 minutes, skimming occasionally.

For **vegetable stock**, see page 77.

Brown sauce, thickened gravies

Brown sauce is basic to a professional kitchen but it also turns up at home as thickened gravy, the much-loved accompaniment to mashed potato, roast meats and poultry. Brown sauce, whether the traditional slowly simmered espagnole based on a roux of flour and oil, or the more modern veal stock thickened with starch, is a test of culinary skill involving multiple ingredients and long simmering. Whisking should be done with discretion, just enough to prevent sticking. Too much can froth and cloud brown sauces. Flavourings are always added to the basic sauce, leading for example to Madeira sauce, charcutière (with reduced white wine, shallot and gherkin pickles) and bordelaise (with reduced red wine, shallot and bone marrow).

GLAZES

Meat, poultry and fish glaze is made by boiling down stock to a syrupy consistency (just a teaspoonful packs powerful flavour). 2 litres/3½ pints of stock will produce 250 ml/8 fl glaze. Ensure the original stock has plenty of gelatine from simmering bones. When cold, glaze sets and will keep, refrigerated, for several months.

STAGES IN COOKING

▼ CONSISTENCY TOO THIN – looks pale; scarcely thickened and runs quickly off surface of spoon or plate; lacks taste.

▼ CONSISTENCY TOO THICK – muddy colour; texture sticky, generously coating a spoon or plate.

▲ PERFECT – glossy, light to deep mahogany colour (darker for red meats and game); very lightly coats a spoon or plate; flavour intense and well balanced.

Unthickened gravies

Good unthickened gravy, often called by its french name *jus*, is made from the caramelized juices that coagulate on the bottom of the roasting or frying pan. These are deglazed (dissolved) with stock, wine or water. If the juices are not well browned, cook them in the pan before adding liquid. Meat or poultry juices include fat, which helps thicken gravy, but tip off all but 1-2 tablespoons before deglazing.

STAGES IN PREPARATION

▼ **PERFECT** – golden brown colour (darker for red meats and game), full-bodied flavour, slightly thickened as juices emulsify when reduced.

▲ **FAT SEPARATED** heavy layer of fat separates from darker juices beneath.

Pork fillet with muscat wine and dried cranberries

Pork fillet can be tied with string to form medallions of meat, ideal for pan-frying to serve with this sweet-and-sour gravy.

SERVES 4

- 2 pork fillets (about 750 g/1½ pounds), trimmed
- 1 teaspoon ground cinnamon
- salt and pepper
- 15 g/½ oz butter
- 1 tablespoon oil
- 60 g/2 oz dried cranberries
- 250 ml/8 fl oz sweet white muscat wine
- 250 ml/8 fl oz brown beef or veal stock
- 1 tablespoon redcurrant jelly
- squeeze of lemon juice

Lay the fillets head to tail and tie them together with 8 pieces of string at even intervals to make a cylinder. Cut between each piece of string to make 8 medallions about 4 cm/1½ inches thick. Season them with cinnamon, salt and pepper.

Heat the butter and oil in a frying pan until foaming. Add the medallions and sauté until brown, 3-5 minutes. Turn them over, lower heat and leave until browned and just cooked to taste, 5-7 minutes. Transfer to a plate and keep warm.

Discard all but a teaspoon of fat from the pan. Add the cranberries, wine and stock, and boil until reduced by half, stirring to dissolve pan juices, 10-12 minutes. Add the redcurrant jelly and lemon juice, and stir until dissolved. Taste and adjust the seasoning.

Add the medallions to the sauce in the pan and reheat for 1 minute. Discard the strings, arrange medallions on 4 warmed plates and spoon over the sauce. Serve at once.

Hollandaise sauce

To ensure that hollandaise is thick and rich enough to act as a coating, be sure the foundation mousse of egg yolk and water is well thickened before adding butter – the mousse should hold the trail of the whisk for at least 3 seconds. Since the sauce relies on butter for flavour, use only the best unsalted butter and clarify it to get rid of the whey impurities. Everyone warns of the dangers of curdling hollandaise – it is indeed based on a fragile emulsion (page 127) and must be cooked and kept warm over very gentle heat. Never let it get more than hand-hot. Some cooks like to use a water bath, though I find a heavy pan sufficient protection. Even if the worst happens, there are several ways to restore hollandaise and possibly the most effective is demonstrated below.

STAGES IN COOKING

▼ **CONSISTENCY TOO THIN** – frothy consistency; lacks body and falls very easily from spoon; flavour faint.

▼ **CURDLED** – butter separates, depositing curds of cooked egg.

▲ **PERFECT** – rich consistency, sauce holds trail of whisk for 10-15 seconds; flavour is delicate, rich with light touch of lemon.

BÉARNAISE SAUCE

Béarnaise sauce, named after the feisty French province of Béarn, is a pungent version of delicate hollandaise. Flavour is piquant rather than mild, with a reduction of tarragon vinegar, tarragon stems and shallot replacing the water used in hollandaise.

Boil this reduction down well so the flavour is concentrated. The texture should be thick and rich, stiffer than hollandaise. To achieve this, before adding melted butter, the basic egg yolk mousse must be cooked until it holds the trail of the whisk for at least 15 seconds. Once the sauce is strained, to give it a final boost chopped tarragon and ground black pepper are added — be sure both are fresh. If the flavour is flat, try a squeeze of lemon juice and a pinch of cayenne. Béarnaise can curdle, just like hollandaise, and is saved in the same way.

Don't limit béarnaise to classic fillet steak and lamb chops, but try it with poached or grilled fish, like turbot and salmon, and even with duck.

▼ **PERFECT** – whisk leaves clear trail through sauce on base of pan for 10-15 seconds; texture creamy and just drops easily from spoon; flavour is assertive, fragrant with tarragon.

▲ RESTORING CURDLED HOLLANDAISE:
cool pan at once by dipping base in cold water. Add an ice cube to the sauce and whisk beside the cube, gradually working the curdled sauce into the melting cube to re-establish an emulsion.

White butter sauce & other butter sauces

Like hollandaise and béarnaise, white butter sauce relies on an emulsion (see page 127) for its consistency – but it is even more delicate as the milk solids and whey in the butter act as the emulsifier. (So butter sauce can't be made with clarified butter, from which the whey has been removed.) As always, the key is to establish the emulsion right from the start by vigorously whisking in a small amount of cold butter. Some cooks add a spoonful of double cream as an additional emulsifier – purists protest a loss of flavour, but it works. Keep a butter sauce warm on a rack over gently steaming water, but not for too long. If it separates, simply serve the sauce as a deliciously seasoned melted butter.

STAGES IN COOKING

▼ **CONSISTENCY TOO THIN** – almost transparent and scarcely coats spoon.

▲ **PERFECT** – lightly coats a spoon and clear trail is left when finger is drawn across back of spoon; flavouring ingredients evenly blended (sometimes strained out); flavour delicate, well balanced, with lingering hint of shallot, wine and vinegar.

Steamed sea bass
with fennel butter sauce

In Provence, pastis, the local anise liqueur, is accorded a respect generally reserved for Cognac. Here it boosts the fennel flavour. This recipe is also good with hake or sea trout.

SERVES 4
4 sea bass fillets (about 750 g/1 1/2 pounds), with skin
salt and pepper

FOR THE COURT BOUILLON
1 onion, spiked with 1 clove
1 carrot, sliced
1 tablespoon fennel seeds
bouquet garni
250 ml/8 fl oz white wine

FOR FENNEL BUTTER SAUCE
250 g/8 oz cold butter, cut into pieces
2 shallots, finely chopped
1 teaspoon fennel seed
125 ml/4 fl oz white wine
2 tablespoons pastis or other anise liqueur

Put all the court bouillon ingredients in the base of a steamer with 500 ml/16 fl oz water, cover and simmer until fragrant, 15-20 minutes.

Set the seasoned fish fillets skin side up on the steamer rack, put the rack over the court bouillon and cover. Steam until done to taste, 10-12 minutes. Remove the fish and keep warm. Strain the steaming liquid into a medium pan and boil until reduced to 2-3 tablespoons of syrupy glaze, 7-10 minutes.

Meanwhile, make the fennel butter sauce: in a medium pan, melt 30 g/1 oz of the butter, add the shallots and fennel seeds, and sauté until the shallot is soft but not browned, 1-2 minutes. Stir in the wine and half the pastis and simmer until reduced to about 2 tablespoons. Whisk in the remaining butter a few pieces at a time, working on and off the heat so the butter softens and thickens the sauce without melting to oil. Strain the sauce into the pan of fish glaze, crushing the shallots to extract their juices. Whisk sauce and glaze together, then stir in the remaining liqueur. Taste and adjust the seasoning.

Spoon pools of the sauce on 4 warmed serving plates. Set a piece of fish on top, skin side up, and serve at once, passing the remaining sauce separately.

▼ SEPARATED – butter separates to top of sauce, leaving flavourings at bottom.

Mayonnaise

Mayonnaise is said to be tricky and it helps to know why. For its satiny rich consistency, mayonnaise depends on an emulsion (opposite) of vinegar, oil and raw egg yolk – 175 ml/6 fl oz of oil per egg yolk are standard proportions. Several conditions are needed for this emulsion to form. First, all the ingredients must be at room temperature; if the eggs come from the refrigerator, you may need to warm them and the bowl. Whisk the egg yolks and seasonings with a teaspoon of vinegar or lemon juice for at least a minute before you add the oil, first drop by drop and then in a trickle. (You can use an immersion blender or hand-held electric mixer.) Without this small amount of liquid, the egg yolks and oil will not emulsify. Once the emulsion is formed and the mayonnaise starts to thicken, you should have no trouble and be rewarded by a mayonnaise so thick it will hold a spoon upright. Given the hazards of raw egg yolks, refrigerate your mayonnaise and use it within 24 hours.

STAGES IN PREPARATION

▼ **PERFECT MEDIUM** – holds mark of whisk; glossy, cream colour; vinegar and other flavourings nicely balance richness of oil.

▼ **SEPARATED** – pours easily from a spoon; coarse-textured, with eggs clearly separated from oil.

▲ **PERFECT THICK** – holds a whisk upright; colour a clear golden; flavour pungent.

Vinaigrette

'Be a prodigal with the oil, a miser with the vinegar and whisk like the devil himself' runs an adage on vinaigrette dressing, and I couldn't agree more. Standard proportions for vinaigrette are three parts oil to one vinegar, but I vary them all the time depending on the inherent strength of the oil or vinegar. A good vinaigrette dressing should be lightly emulsified by vigorous whisking so it coats salad leaves or whatever food it accompanies – a spoonful of Dijon-style mustard or cream will help the oil and vinegar combine, but is not essential. On standing, the dressing separates, but can easily be recombined by whisking. Don't refrigerate vinaigrette as the oil will congeal. Careful seasoning is key to good vinaigrette and the theory that salt will not dissolve in a dressing once the oil is added is nonsense.

EMULSIONS & EMULSIFIERS

An emulsion is formed when two substances that would normally separate, for example oil and vinegar, are combined to a smooth, lightly thickened mixture. Sauces which rely on an emulsion include hollandaise, béarnaise, white butter sauce, mayonnaise and vinaigrette.

Several factors help to create an emulsion. One is to add an emulsifier – an ingredient that helps other ingredients to combine in this way. Common examples are egg yolks (hollandaise, béarnaise and mayonnaise), Dijon-style mustard (mayonnaise and vinaigrette), the milk solids in butter and cream (butter sauces), spices and herbs.

Next is vigorous whisking, typically adding one liquid to the emulsifier, starting drop by drop. It is crucial to establish the emulsion right at the beginning. Once off to a good start – you can tell by the slight but perceptible thickening of the mixture – the liquid may then be added more quickly.

Other factors which help an emulsion to form include following proportions carefully, and having the ingredients and utensils at the right (usually room) temperature. It is difficult, for example, to make mayonnaise with eggs which have come straight from the refrigerator.

▲ **PERFECT** *right*– lightly thickened and ingredients smooth and emulsified; flavour balanced and seasoning vivid.

THIN, NOT EMULSIFIED *left* – oil and vinegar lose emulsion and form separate layers.

Tomato sauces & cooked salsas

Italian cooks are masters of tomato sauce, so it's surprising that they developed a passion for the tomato barely 150 years ago. Only in Italy do you find such an array of tomato sauces, whether for pasta and pizza, or to accompany fish, poultry, meat and vegetables. Simplest is a coulis of fresh tomatoes seasoned with salt, pepper and fresh herbs, so lightly cooked it is only just hot. Marinara-style sauces are more full-bodied, backed with onion and garlic. At the far end of the spectrum come terracotta-gold essences of tomato so concentrated that a teaspoonful conveys a whole fruit.

The French, like the Italians, will often cook a simply flavoured tomato sauce down until nearly all the moisture has evaporated. This preparation is called *tomates concassées* because the tomatoes are first peeled, seeded and chopped. Elsewhere, cooks may approach tomatoes differently, for example adding hot chilli and roasting the tomatoes with garlic and onion for a cooked Mexican salsa. Whatever their name or origin, the same criteria of quality apply to all cooked tomato sauces: they should be full-flavoured without being too sweet or acid, richly coloured and as thin or thick as you require.

STAGES IN COOKING

▼ **PERFECT MEDIUM** – slightly chunky, drops easily from spoon but too thick to pour; rich, vivid colour; flavour mellow and concentrated.

▲ **PERFECT THICK** – liquid evaporated so sauce clearly holds mark of spoon without being sticky; flavour intense but not salty or acid; colour earthy.

Fresh salsas

A good fresh salsa is crisp, crunchy and bursting with taste. The colourful ingredients – green, red and gold – should say 'New World'. Salsa is not just the indispensable accompaniment to tacos, empanadas, burritos and other dishes from its native Mexico. Consider it a versatile condiment on the lines of a relish to accompany all manner of grilled and sautéed fish, poultry and meats, rather than the traditional smooth sauce designed to act as a coating.

The flavour of a fresh salsa must be forceful, even crude, so typically it is based on chopped sweet onion, diced cucumber, celery, radish, jícama, sweet pepper and chilli. Typical herbs include coriander, basil, thyme and dill. To bind all of this, chopped tomato is customary, but other juicy fruits such as avocado, mango, peach or plum may take its place. The mixture may be chopped coarsely or finely, to your taste, but do be careful not to bruise delicate herbs such as basil or coriander. I like to leave flavours to mellow for an hour or two, even overnight, but don't overdo it, as some fruits – notably stone fruits such as peach – will discolour and lose their aroma.

▲ *from left to right*
WATERY – ingredients flabby, liquid separates at bottom of salsa; colour faded and flavour flat.
PERFECT FINE – ingredients finely chopped; flavour lively.
PERFECT CHUNKY – ingredients coarsely chopped, though small enough to blend; individual flavours more pronounced.

VEGETABLE-THICKENED SAUCES

In medieval times, pulses and grains were included in stews, then for centuries vegetable thickeners fell into disuse, only to be revived some years ago. A pulpy effect is perfectly acceptable for most vegetable sauces, particularly when part of a meat or poultry stew. For a smoother consistency, purée the sauce, and possibly strain it to remove fibres.
PERFECT (left) – sauce coats back of spoon, consistency rich; flavour pungent or aromatic.
GRAINY (right) – texture coarse; liquid may seep at edges of sauce; flavour undeveloped.

Pastry cream & thickened custard sauces

Pastry cream often acts as a medium to enrich and thicken other ingredients, so consistency is all-important. For almost all uses, pastry cream should be thick enough to hold a shape but not so sticky as to be unpleasant on the tongue. Standard proportions are 3 egg yolks, 50 g/1¾ oz sugar and 10 g/1½ tablespoons flour or 7 g/1 tablespoon cornflour for each 250 ml/8 fl oz of milk. With more milk, pastry cream becomes a custard. Constant whisking of both pastry cream and thickened custard sauce ensures they thicken evenly, and a heavy pan lessens the risk of scorching. Given the ingredients of egg yolk and milk, you might think pastry cream or thickened custard sauce would be liable to curdle. However, the mixture contains enough flour or starch to be boiled without danger of separating. When thickened with flour, pastry cream is smooth and soft; with cornflour it is glossy, but can be sticky; while with potato starch it is very light.

STAGES IN COOKING

▶ **PERFECT PASTRY CREAM**
– glossy and very smooth; when hot, holds mark of whisk for 3-5 seconds but still falls easily from spoon; delicate golden colour dotted with vanilla seeds; flavour perfumed and rich, with no trace of flour or starch; when cooled, thickens just enough to hold shape.

▼ **PERFECT THICKENED CUSTARD SAUCE** – glossy and very smooth; coats a spoon and pours off spoon in a steady stream; flavour delicate, usually of vanilla.

◀ PASTRY CREAM TOO THICK – when hot, pastry cream is sticky and holds a shape; when cold, it is stiff and glutinous; flavour is floury.

Filo millefeuille with raspberries and light pastry cream

SERVES 4-6

4 sheets of filo pastry
45 g/1½ oz butter
3 tablespoons honey
175 g/6 oz raspberries

FOR THE PASTRY CREAM
250 ml/8 fl oz milk
1 vanilla pod, split
3 egg yolks
50 g/1¾ oz sugar
1½ tablespoons flour

FOR THE CHANTILLY CREAM
250 ml/8 fl oz double cream
2 tablespoons icing sugar
1 tablespoon brandy

Make the pastry cream: scald milk in a pan with vanilla pod, cover and leave to infuse off heat for 5-10 minutes. Meanwhile, beat egg yolks with sugar until thick and light. Stir in flour. Whisk milk into egg mix and return to pan. Cook over a low heat, whisking constantly, until it boils and thickens. Simmer, stirring, for 1 or 2 minutes. Strain into a bowl. Rinse vanilla for use again. Rub surface of pastry cream with butter or press cling film on top to prevent a skin forming and chill.

Preheat oven to 230°C/450°F/gas8. Brush baking sheet with butter. Heat honey and remaining butter until melted. Lay a sheet of pastry on prepared baking sheet and brush with the honey butter. Lay a second sheet on top and brush again. Repeat until all 4 sheets are used, brushing top of last layer with honey butter. With a sharp knife or pastry wheel, cut filo layers lengthwise in 3 strips, trimming edges. Cut each strip in 6 pieces to make 18 rectangles. Bake until golden and glaze on top begins to caramelize, 5-6 minutes.

The layers will puff and separate slightly. Transfer to a rack and let cool.

Make Chantilly cream: whip double cream until it holds a soft peak. Add sugar and brandy and continue whipping until holding a soft peak.

When pastry cream is cold, whisk briefly to lighten. Fold in Chantilly cream. Spread 1-2 heaped tablespoons of this over one rectangle of filo. Top

with a few raspberries and set a second rectangle, slightly askew, on top. Add more pastry cream and raspberries and top with a last rectangle of filo, setting it askew. Assemble remaining millefeuilles in same way. Transfer to a serving plate and sprinkle some berries around the edge. Serve chilled.

Custard sauce

The best custard, or *crème anglaise* to give it its French name, is home-made from whole milk, thickened with egg yolks and sweetened with sugar – standard proportions are 500 ml/16 fl oz milk, 5 egg yolks and 50 g/1¾ oz sugar. Flavour is easily tainted, so use fresh, previously unopened milk. Sometimes a light thickener is added – see Pastry Cream and Thickened Custard Sauces (page 130). The main danger when making it is curdling – it thickens at 82°C/180°F, and overcooks at only 6°C/10°F more, so must never be allowed to boil. It will only thicken slightly, with less body than flour-based custard. To spread the heat evenly, I use a heavy pan, preferably made of copper, and stir steadily with a wooden spoon over low to medium heat. Use a water bath if you like, but it will take much longer. Egg yolks and sugar can be lightly beaten before adding the heated milk, but during cooking do not be tempted to whisk the custard itself. The aim is a smooth rich finish.

STAGES IN COOKING

▼ **CONSISTENCY TOO THIN** – same consistency as milk; custard runs together when finger is drawn across back of spoon.

▼ **CURDLED** – milk separates, leaving egg curds.

▲ **PERFECT** – creamy, smooth and clear trail is left when finger is drawn across back of spoon; flavour is delicate, perfumed with vanilla.

Sweet sabayon sauce

Sweet sabayon sauce is closely related to the fluffy Italian dessert zabaglione, made with egg yolks, sugar and Marsala. Perhaps sabayon's most popular use is to coat fresh fruits, particularly berries and orange segments, then to brown them as a gratin. Given its generous content of liqueur or fruit juice (standard proportions are 1 tablespoon sugar and 2 tablespoons liquid for each egg yolk), sweet sabayon sauce is inclined to curdle. Whisk it vigorously, using very low heat so thickening does not even start for 2-3 minutes. With regret, I must admit that an electric mixer is not a good substitute for hard work by hand with a balloon whisk in a copper or metal bowl. Do not heat the sauce too much – the bottom of the bowl should never be very hot to the touch. Serve sabayon as soon as you can, preferably still warm.

STAGES IN COOKING

▼ **CONSISTENCY TOO THIN** – pours very easily and lacks richness.

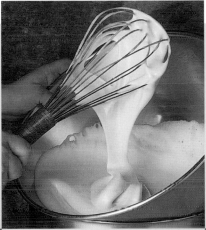

▼ **CURDLED** – thin, coarse consistency with tiny curds of egg visible; texture is slightly granular on the tongue.

▲ **PERFECT** – smooth, fluffy and rich, holds ribbon trail of whisk 10 seconds; flavour is delicate, aromatic with liqueur, wine or fruit juice. Note: if whisked until cool, sabayon will hold 10-15 minutes without separating, but not longer.

Fruit coulis & purées

The name 'coulis' comes from the french *couler*, meaning 'to flow', and implies a puréed sauce, used to describe both savoury and sweet preparations. Consistency should be pourable but somewhat thicker than a coating sauce. A fruit purée is even thicker than a coulis, firm enough to hold a shape. Fruit coulis and purées may be fresh or cooked. Both should be vivid in flavour and colour, with a smooth or slightly chunky texture free of fibre. You need an assertive fruit, such as apricot, peach, mango, pineapple, cranberry, raspberry, blackberry or strawberry. For both coulis and purée, I like to work the fruit pulp briefly in a processor or with an immersion blender so a bit of texture is left, but it is equally correct to strain them for a smoother finish. In any case, some fruits such as raspberries must be strained to remove seeds or fibre. Remember that some fresh fruits discolour very quickly and must be generously doused with lemon juice.

STAGES IN PREPARATION

▼ **CONSISTENCY TOO THIN** – coulis or purée watery, lacks body; easy to pour; colour and flavour muted.

▼ **PERFECT PURÉE** – texture even, possibly coarse but not fibrous; purée thick enough to leave a ribbon trail, but still just falls from spoon; flavour intense.

▲ **PERFECT COULIS** – texture smooth, glossy but less emulsified than strained sauce; coulis generously coats a spoon but pours easily; colour vivid and flavour rich.

Cooked fruit sauces

Similar as they are on the dessert plate, a cooked fruit sauce gives a different impression from a coulis. Where a coulis is vibrant, the flavour of a fruit sauce is more complex and mellow. Texture can be as thick as the apple sauce commonly served with pancakes, or semi-transparent and so thin that the sauce scarcely veils the food beneath. Fruits should be pungent: apricot, blackberry, cherry, cranberry, lemon, orange, plum, redcurrant and blackcurrant are typical. Often they are cooked in syrup and may or may not be puréed. When they need thickening, a starch which cooks to be transparent and glossy is best, such as cornflour, arrowroot or potato starch. By no means all cooked fruit sauces are intended for dessert. Apple sauce with pork and cranberry sauce with roast turkey spring to mind.

STAGES IN COOKING

CONSISTENCY TOO THIN – watery, almost transparent, lacks colour and taste.

▼ **GRAINY** – uneven, sometimes gluey texture, often muddy colour.

▲ **PERFECT** – very smooth and lightly coats a spoon; colour brilliant and glossy; flavour concentrated and refreshing.

Chocolate sauces

A reliable recipe for chocolate sauce will always call for enough liquid to melt the chocolate without danger of seizing (see opposite). In chocolate sauce this is caused by too little liquid – 1½ teaspoons of liquid per 30 g/1 oz chocolate is the bare minimum to keep melted chocolate smooth. When simmering a sauce to the right consistency for a given dish, you may by accident boil too far. Another mishap can occur if hot or cold liquid is poured on melted chocolate and stirred – the chocolate may briefly seize so the sauce looks lumpy and flecked. If simmered it will become smooth, so do not worry. Whether a recipe calls for plain, dark, milk or white chocolate, look for reputable brands made without cocoa substitutes or additives (other than the milk added to milk chocolate). A cold sauce to go with mousses, sponge cake or poached fruit, should be thinner than a hot one for profiteroles, soufflés, etc. Fudge sauce for ice cream is the thickest of all.

STAGES IN COOKING

▼ **PERFECT** – rich-flavoured, glossy; whether hot or cold, lightly coats a spoon.

▲ **PERFECT FUDGE** – very thick and rich; sets on contact with cold surface such as ice cream.

Melting chocolate

There are dozens of types and flavours of chocolate, each with varying amounts of cocoa butter. The higher the cocoa butter, the more easily chocolate softens and melts. Some recipes may call for couverture, often called 'dipping' or 'coating' chocolate. This is the ideal confectioners' chocolate as it has a high cocoa butter content, varying between 35 and 50 per cent, with no padding of cheaper vegetable oil. Melting is also affected by sugar content, particularly in sweet and milk chocolates.

The main problem when melting chocolate is 'seizing', a term describing chocolate which suddenly stiffens and becomes grainy. This will happen if a few drops of water come in contact with the chocolate – a damp bowl can be the cause, or steam from a water bath. Seizing can be reversed, but the chocolate will never be quite so glossy. More serious is the seizing caused by overheating, which makes the cocoa butter separate from the cocoa solids. It cannot be recombined.

After chopping, chocolate can be melted by warming it in a double boiler or in a bowl or plate placed over hot water (about 48°C/120°F); a microwave also does a good job. Don't stir at once, but leave the warmth to penetrate and when you see the sharp outlines of the chocolate blur, it's nearly melted. Begin stirring gently every 15-20 seconds until smooth – consistency will vary, with unsweetened chocolate the thinnest, milk chocolate the thickest. Take particular care with milk and white chocolates – a lower heat of around 37°C/100°F is best. Once melted, chocolate may be tempered – a heating and cooling technique which makes it more malleable and glossy.

STAGES IN PREPARATION

▼ **PERFECT** – chocolate just thin enough to pour, smooth, very glossy and even-textured when stirred; colour rich, varying with type of chocolate.

▲ **SEIZED** – chocolate suddenly stiffens to rough, lumpy texture; oily cocoa butter may separate to surface; looks granular and lacks gloss. To remedy, take off heat, dry any beads of steam on bowl and stir in 1-2 teaspoons vegetable oil a little at a time until chocolate is smooth again.

Fruit

The less you do to a fine fruit, the better it is. What can equal the heady aroma of pears poached in sugar syrup with vanilla and spices or an apple baked with honey or sautéed in a bit of butter and sugar to a rich caramel brown? Firm fruits such as apple are also good deep-fried as fritters, but only the juiciest like peach or pineapple grill well. I find that a fruit's flavour can be quite transformed by cooking – a poached or baked apricot, for example, can be a revelation. Always buy the ripest and most aromatic fruit you can. Good cooking cannot compensate for lack of taste in fruit picked too soon.

For many dishes, a fruit is cooked when it is tender but still holds its shape. With further cooking, fruits often collapse naturally into purée – this may be deliberate, so don't think of them as necessarily being overcooked. They'll be perfect to serve with ice cream, to flavour cream desserts and sauces or to cook down as preserves.

Sugar, or another sweetener such as honey, is the first and often the only ingredient needed when cooking fruit. Consider its role like that of salt in savoury foods, developing and highlighting taste. The amount you want to add will vary, depending not just on the acidity of the fruit itself but also on its role, whether as an accompaniment to meat or poultry, or as a traditional dessert. Under individual fruits, you'll find suggestions for other flavourings, with spices, sweet wines and liqueurs featuring large. Use your judgement when adding liquid, as juicy fruits will need less.

The characteristic shape and colour of a fruit is decoration in itself, so I like to leave them whole whenever possible. Portions are easy to judge by eye and intuition. Cut pieces should suit a fruit's personality – crescents for apples, hemispheres for apricots and plums, and flower-petal slashes for figs to display their pretty pink interior. The dullest day must surely be cheered by a pile of fruit on the kitchen table, so I hope you'll read on with pleasure. Life, after all, is just a bowl of cherries!

GRILLED PEACH AND STRAWBERRY KEBABS, PAGE 145

Apples

By and large, apples fall into three categories: there are those which hold their shape during cooking and so are good for baking in their skins, sautéing in slices or poaching in syrup – Golden Delicious is the most common. Other varieties such as Granny Smith fall apart quickly when heated and are ideal for purée and apple sauce. In pies, either firm or soft apples can be used. A few apples are good only for the table, losing their taste and crisp texture all too easily if they are subjected to heat – Fuji, Gala and Red Delicious for instance. We're lucky to have more and more varieties of apple appearing in the markets now, some new and others a revival of old, half-forgotten favourites. How they will behave in the kitchen can be a mystery, so look out for information from the grower. As they discolour readily, always cut apples just before you plan to cook them or toss the cut pieces in lemon juice.

STAGES IN COOKING

▼ **UNDERCOOKED AND PALE** – resistant when pierced with point of a knife; if cut, centre is hard and opaque; whether whole, sliced or chopped, apple holds a firm shape.

▼ **OVERCOOKED** – very soft, shape disintegrating into purée; if sautéed or grilled, edges often scorched; if whole, apple collapses; fresh flavour mellowed. For purée or apple sauce, apples should be cooked to this stage.

▲ **PERFECT** – tender when pierced with point of a knife; flesh looks translucent, not opaque; if sliced or chopped, pieces hold shape; if baked in skin, apple is slightly puffed, still holding shape; colour is pale or caramelized, depending on recipe; flavour tangy and fresh.

Upside-down apple pie *Tarte des Demoiselles Tatin*

SERVES 8-10
175 g/6 oz butter
400 g/14 oz sugar
2.8 kg/6 pounds firm apples

**30-35-cm/12-14-inch heavy-based deep
    frying pan**

FOR THE FRENCH PIE PASTRY
200 g/6¹/₂ oz flour
100 g/3¹/₄ oz butter
1 egg yolk
¹/₂ teaspoon salt
45 ml/1¹/₂ fl oz water, more if needed

Make pastry: sift flour on a work surface and make well in centre. Pound butter with rolling pin to soften. Put butter, egg yolk, salt and water in well. With fingers, work moist ingredients until well mixed. Draw in flour and work in other ingredients with fingers of both hands until coarse crumbs form. If crumbs very dry, add 1-2 tablespoons more water. Press dough into ball. Lightly flour work surface. Blend dough by pushing it away from you with heel of your hand, then gathering it up until very smooth and peels away from work surface in one piece, 1-2 minutes. Shape into ball, wrap and chill for, at least 30 minutes. Preheat oven to 220°C/425°F/gas7.

Melt butter in the pan and sprinkle with sugar. Cook over medium heat until sugar starts to caramelize. Stir, then continue cooking to a medium caramel (it may separate). Let cool.

Peel, halve and core apples. Arrange halves upright, cut side at right angles to pan edge in concentric circles on caramel to fill pan completely and fit snugly. Cook over high heat until deep golden caramel, 15-20 minutes. The apples will make juice, which must evaporate before they'll caramelize. Turn apples over and cook 10-15 minutes more.

When apples cooked, let cool slightly. Roll out pastry to circle slightly larger than pan. Set dough on apples to cover completely, quickly tucking in at edges. Bake until pastry firm and slightly browned, 20-25 minutes. Let cool in pan. Turn out on a large plate just before serving.

Pears & quinces

Many varieties of pear cook well, holding their shape in gentle heat. Common cooking pears include Anjou and Williams. The only one I'd avoid is the juicy Comice as its melting texture does not hold up well. Looking like a craggy yellow pear, the quince is an old fruit that is coming back into style. It cannot be eaten raw and needs very thorough cooking for up to three or four hours with plenty of sugar until the crunchy flesh softens and turns a beguiling deep pink. Whatever the flavouring, pears and quinces must be peeled for cooking and moistened generously with liquid (sautéed pears are an exception). They discolour quickly, so a rub with lemon is a necessity. Pears are fragile and easily bruised: if picked too soon, the flesh around the core may darken before or after cooking. When poaching a pear whole, scoop out the core from the base with a pointed teaspoon; for easier handling, leave the stem.

COBBLERS AND OTHER FRUIT PUDDINGS

Crumble, streusel, gratin, cobbler – when you think about it, there are a multitude of toppings designed to be baked on a layer of fruit. That's because the results are so delicious. The topping, whether crisp, crumbling or cake-like, is invariably rich and sweet. Crumble (also called a crisp) is typical, a combination of butter, sugar and flour, often with chopped nuts or oatmeal, that is baked on top of fresh or stewed fruit.

Streusel is the German version of crumble, often with a cake base beneath the fruit, resulting in a three-layered finish. In France, the term 'gratin' covers any browned fruit pudding, while cobbler is a catch-all. The finish of a cobbler is juicy, rather than crisp. Cobbler may be topped with a dough resembling a sablé biscuit, or with scone dough, or with a cakey batter, or even with pie pastry though I'd call this a top-crust pie.

Cobbler is just the start of the toppings created by American cooks – the virtuosi of the field. A betty is topped with buttered breadcrumbs, a buckle uses cake batter, and a grunt is covered with scone dough soft enough to drop from a spoon. A pandowdy refers to a pie pastry topping which is partially baked, then slashed and pushed down into the fruit so it finishes to be crisp and flavoured with juice.

How about the fruit? Here I hold strong views: fruit to be baked with a topping must be tart and juicy to balance the sweet crust, and I add little or no sweetener or flavouring to the fruit unless the topping is plain (scone dough for instance).

▲ **PERFECT** – tender when pierced with point of a knife; flesh looks opaque, with no translucent centre when cut (texture of quince always remains slightly granular); fruit pieces hold shape; colour is pale or lightly caramelized depending on recipe; flavour fresh (for pears) or fragrant (for quinces). Note: tests for under- and overcooked pear and quince are the same as for apple (page 140).

Apricots & plums

Apricots and plums can be the best or the worst of fruit – juicy, perfumed, brilliantly coloured, or a dreadful disappointment. We've all had apricots that are tasteless from lack of sun, or plums that pucker the mouth. Plums are the easier to remedy, as sugar will at least add sweetness if not depth of flavour. Apricots are more difficult; if they are bland I'd suggest poaching them in a lively syrup. Plums are more aggressive – with no extra help you can rely on them to assert their flavour in all manner of pies and puddings. Both apricots and plums make charming open tarts, halved or quartered to arrange in a flower pattern, and then baked cut side up so the juices evaporate and the pastry remains crisp. Ripe fruits are easy to halve with a knife, following the indentation, then twisting the halves apart, but unripe they tend to cling to the stone. Sprinkle apricots with lemon juice or they discolour rapidly. Both apricots and plums bake and grill well.

STAGES IN COOKING

▼ **PERFECT** – tender when pierced with a two-pronged fork; flesh translucent; whether whole or pieces, fruit holds shape; colour bright and flavour strong.

▲ **PERFECT FOR PURÉE** – flesh disintegrating into purée; very soft if pierced with a two-pronged fork; flavour mellowed; colour slightly faded.

Nectarines & peaches

Handle nectarines and peaches carefully as they bruise easily. Once cut, they discolour rapidly, so rub with lemon juice and then immerse them in liquid or cook them at once. Look out for the designation 'freestone' or 'clingstone', a key to how peaches behave when you try to halve them (cut along the indentation and around the fruit, then give a quick twist). The skin also clings more firmly to clingstone fruit. To loosen the skin of peaches, immerse them for 10-15 seconds in boiling water, then transfer to cold water and peel. When poaching in syrup, peaches are peeled after cooking and you'll find a pretty pink blush has formed under the skin. Nectarines can be hard to peel even when blanched, but their skin is thin so I often don't bother.

STAGES IN COOKING

▼ **PERFECT** – tender when pierced with two-pronged fork, but fruit still firm enough to be lifted; if whole or halved, fruit still holds shape; surface shiny with juice; fruit is translucent, with no opaque centre when cut; colour clear and flavour fresh and fruity.

▲ **OVERCOOKED AND WOOLLY** – shape slumped; juices run into pan; fruit is very soft if pierced with fork, and falls apart when lifted; colour and flavour dull.

Grilled peach and strawberry kebabs

Fruit kebabs can be grilled indoors, or they make the ideal dessert for a summer barbecue. I don't bother to peel the peaches, as high heat softens the skins in any case.

SERVES 4

4 large peaches (about 500 g/1 pound)
12 large strawberries
45 g/1¹/₂ oz melted butter
100 g/3¹/₄ oz sugar

four 25-cm/10-inch wooden skewers

Preheat the grill. Put the skewers in a dish of cold water to soak so they do not scorch during grilling.

Cut the peaches in half, using the indentations on one side as a guide. With both hands, give a quick, sharp twist to the halves to loosen them from the stones. Cut each half in half again, or in thirds if the pieces are large. Hull the strawberries, rinsing them only if they are sandy.

Drain the skewers. Thread 3 strawberries and 4 peach quarters alternately on each skewer. Brush the kebabs generously with melted butter and roll in sugar so the fruit is thoroughly covered. Arrange the kebabs on a grill rack lined with foil.

Grill about 7.5 cm/3 inches from the heat, until the fruit is tender and caramelized, turning once, 4-6 minutes on each side. Serve on the skewers.

Figs

Figs are a favourite with contemporary chefs, valued for their pretty shape and deep pink interior in dishes such as pork medallions with figs in red wine, and foie gras with roast figs. More traditional ideas include figs simmered in rum syrup or orange juice and ginger. The simplest way to cook them is to bake or poach them, whether whole, quartered or thickly sliced. The two common types of fig – black- or green-skinned – are interchangeable. Leave the skin, both for colour and to hold the soft flesh in place.

STAGES IN COOKING

▲ **PERFECT** – fruit flexible but still holding shape; tender when pierced with point of a knife; juices starting to run; flavour mellow.

Cherries

Cherries are one of the few fruits which remain seasonal, an instant evocation of the summer to come. Varieties divide into cookers and eaters and you'll know which by tasting – cooking cherries are almost inedibly acid. They are often, though not necessarily, bright red. These are the best for classics such as cherry pie or duck with cherries, as their tang is potent even when laced generously with sugar. Other recipes like black cherry jam rely on sweeter fruit for a more mellow taste – Bing are the most common variety. Stones are a nuisance when cooking with cherries. If you leave them, the fruit has more taste as the stones contain a trace of almond flavour. Removing them takes time, even with the tool designed for the purpose, and the fruit then tends to disintegrate. In many recipes, the choice is yours. Be warned that cherries, like berries, can overcook and fall apart in a minute or two if the heat is high.

▲ **PERFECT** – cherries tender, just starting to lose shape; juices running generously; colour bright and flavour tart.

CANDIED FRUITS

Fruit is candied by simmering and soaking it in sugar syrup. The candied whole fruit that appears at Christmas demand multiple soakings and can take several months to candy. However, with a simple candying process you can have candied fruit slices that keep up to a week. Semi-translucent, fragrant strips or julienne of citrus fruits, useful for decoration, are even easier to achieve at home.

Slow, gentle cooking ensures the syrup reaches the centre of the fruit. Keep pieces even and small enough for the syrup to soak thoroughly – whole fruit like cherries must be pricked with a cocktail stick. Bitter fruit, such as citrus peel, should be blanched beforehand. If the syrup is too thick, it will not penetrate thoroughly; if too thin, the fruit scarcely candies to the ideal soft, almost translucent finish.

The rules for sugar cooking apply to candying. When making the syrup, be sure the sugar has completely dissolved before boiling. The sugar may crystallize; if a syrup is stirred or if crystals from the side of the pan or top of the fruit fall into it. A spoonful of glucose or honey, a squeeze of lemon juice or a pinch of cream of tartar helps prevent this.

Berries

For berries, ripeness is all-important, whether in the pan or on the plate. Fragile types like strawberries and raspberries scarcely hold up to cooking at all – often brief maceration in sugar and wine or fruit juice is enough. At the other end of the scale, currants and gooseberries are almost always improved by some gentle simmering with sugar, while cranberries are quite simply inedible when raw. Other berries range between the two extremes. The sugar content of berries can vary enormously with variety and ripeness, so taste one to judge its quality before you start. Many berries are so full of juice that they need no added liquid for cooking. I simply pick over and trim them, avoiding washing if I can. If berries are sandy, rinse them gently with water in a colander, but never leave them to soak. Be aware that they all overcook easily: plump and tender one minute, they can burst or collapse the next, so watch them carefully and use gentle heat.

STAGES IN COOKING

▶ **PERFECT** – berries just tender when tasted, but still holding shape; juices running generously; colour vivid; flavour biting, usually softened by sugar.

◀ **PERFECT WELL-COOKED** – berries very soft and shapes disintegrating to purée; flavour less biting, more concentrated; colours muted. Note: this stage is perfect for berry purées.

FRUIT

Rhubarb

Early in the season, rhubarb may be bright pink and tender, raised in a hot house, but garden rhubarb is likely to be tougher, with thick, bright green stems that must be peeled like those of celery. It is never bland – the acidity of rhubarb can rival that of cranberries, needing plenty of added sugar. Any flavouring must be pungent to make an impact. Watch out for overcooking, as once it is done, rhubarb softens very quickly to become a stringy pulp. I bake rhubarb simply with raspberry or strawberry jam, as it develops plenty of its own juice. In the USA it is also known as the pie plant, and makes a favourite filling for a double crust pie when mixed with strawberries. Rhubarb compote can be a dessert or a pleasant contemporary accompaniment to roast duck and game dishes.

STAGES IN COOKING

▼ **PERFECT** – tender when pierced with a fork; juices running and pieces just starting to lose shape; colour bright and flavour tart but fresh.

▲ **OVERCOOKED** – pieces shrivelled and falling apart when touched with fork; juices running very freely; colour faded and flavour pungent.

Bananas

We don't cook bananas often enough in Europe and North America. Heat develops their taste and allows their somewhat sticky flesh to turn more juicy and fruit-like. For cooking, it's important that bananas be firm rather than fully ripe and soft. When choosing the fruit, the skin should be lightly freckled with brown spots, but never brownish and yielding to your touch. Don't be misled by plantains, which are larger and firmer than bananas and lack the sugar. (Plantains should be treated as a starchy vegetable, and are good baked or deep-fried.) When preparing bananas, leave them whole or cut them in big chunks so they hold their shape. After peeling, they discolour quite quickly, so cook them immediately – for once lemon juice is no remedy as it spoils the rich sweet taste of the fruit.

▲ **PERFECT** – flesh very tender but still holds shape; colour light gold or dark with caramel, depending on recipe; flavour full-bodied and mellow.

Fruit fritters

Fruits are trickier to fry as fritters than vegetables because of their juice, but all the more delicious. Cut the fruit (which should be firm, even slightly under-ripe) into quite generous slices or chunks so they overcook less easily, and dry well before coating. Fruits are invariably fried in batter, as a breadcrumb coating is too heavy and a simple coating of flour doesn't offer sufficient protection. You'll find a light, tempura-style batter is good. Don't be tempted to add much sugar to fritter batter, however, as it scorches quickly in the high heat. I always try a test fritter to gauge fat temperature, thickness of coating and behaviour of the fruit itself. If fritters are acid after frying, just sprinkle with sugar or serve with a sweet sauce. Try to keep flavourings to a minimum as deep-frying wonderfully develops that of the fruit itself. A sprinkling of lemon juice, sugar, liqueur or rum just before the fritters are rushed to the table is often enough.

STAGES IN COOKING

▼ **UNDERCOOKED** – coating pallid, soggy when drained; when cut, fruit often raw and has absorbed fat.

▲ **PERFECT** – coating crisp and golden; when cut, fruit is tender. Fritters a pale to deep gold, crisp and light when drained; fruit evenly coated with batter; fruit flavour is vivid, texture soft or firm but not soggy.

DIPPED AND COATED FRUITS

I said at the beginning of this chapter that, with their lively colours and shapes, fruits are their own decoration. So what better way to display them than with a light coating which still reveals their underlying character? Dipped or coated fruits are delicious with coffee, and form elegant decorations for cakes and desserts.

Half a dozen ideal fruits include cherries, strawberries, grapes and segments of orange and tangerine. Cape gooseberries are particularly pretty, with their papery 'cape' folded back to reveal the golden fruit. The main criterion when choosing fruit for dipping is a firm skin so that juice does not come into contact with the coating – leave stems on cherries and grapes, hulls on strawberries and divide citrus fruits carefully so juice does not leak. Stems are handy for dipping the fruit, or use a toothpick.

Sugar syrup is a popular coating, setting to be clear and crisp. The syrup is boiled to the hard-crack stage (a sugar thermometer should register 146°C/295°F) or to a light caramel at the slightly higher temperature of 160°C/320°F. To coat about 200 g/6½ oz of fruits, you'll need syrup made with 300 g/9¾ oz sugar and 250 ml/8 fl oz water. Have ready a baking sheet lined with greaseproof paper and a bowl of warm water.

When the syrup reaches the right temperature, immerse the base of the pan in the water to stop cooking. Dip the fruits one by one into the hot syrup, letting the excess drain off so a 'foot' does not form when the fruit is set on the paper to harden. Sugar-coated fruits soften after 3-4 hours, particularly in a moist atmosphere. Serve them in paper candy cases.

Fondant icing is an alternative to sugar syrup as a coating, easy to use and readily available commercially – don't think of making your own. Simply warm the fondant with a little sugar syrup so it lightly coats the fruit and dip as for sugar syrup. However, the colour of the fruit is veiled by the white fondant coating. White or dark chocolate has the same disadvantage and is rich as well, so often fruits are half-dipped as a compromise.

For an attractive, frosted coating, fruits may be dipped in lightly beaten egg whites, then rolled in caster sugar and left to dry for an hour. Bunches of redcurrants or blackcurrants and baby grapes are favourites for this treatment and can hold up for 12 hours in an airtight container.

▼ COATING DISINTEGRATING – coating unevenly browned and breaks off into fat; fruit not thoroughly coated, so exposed parts scorch.

Fruit jams

Making jam is really very simple, a matter of achieving the right balance of acid, sugar and pectin so the jam sets just right, with a vivid colour and taste. Acid content is easy to judge by tasting the fruit: if low, you can add more in the form of lemon juice or perhaps a tart apple or two – allow 2 tablespoons juice per 500 g/1 pound of fruit. As for sugar, much depends on the type of fruit and its ripeness – anything from two-thirds to equal parts by volume of sugar to fruit is a good rule of thumb. (Some recipes specify another sweetener such as honey.) Pectin level can be judged by a simple test (opposite). Once sugar is added to the fruit, it must be allowed to dissolve before the jam is brought to the boil. Then it is kept at a rolling boil. Towards the end of cooking, you must skim often and stir so the jam does not boil over or scorch on the base of the pan. The jars must, of course, be sterilized, the contents well sealed and the jam kept in a cool, dry place.

STAGES IN COOKING

▼ **UNDERCOOKED** – jam runs quickly from spoon and froths in pan; sugar thermometer registers under 106°C/220°F.

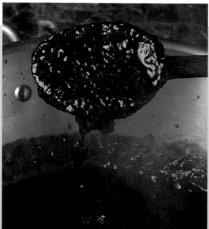

▼ **OVERCOOKED** – jam dark and sticky, clinging to spoon; thermometer registers above 106°C/220°F; colour has brownish tinge; flavour is dense, often smoky with caramel and pan base scorched.

▲ **PERFECT** – jam sheets in even drops from side of spoon on a chilled plate; a few drops of jam set in 3-5 seconds when pushed with a finger; bubbles break more slowly and no longer froth in pan; sugar thermometer registers 106°C/220°F; colour rich, flavour full-bodied with good balance of tart, fruity and sweet.

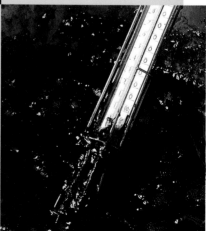

Fruit jellies

Jelly is made by straining the juice from cooked fruit, then boiling it with sugar, just like jam. All the same guidelines apply, particularly the need to balance acid, sugar and pectin. Fruits for jelly must have plenty of flavour and preferably colour too. If the fruit tastes good, sufficient acid is not usually a problem. Sugar depends on the type and ripeness of the fruit; anything from two-thirds to equal parts by volume sugar to fruit juice. Pectin content is particularly important – only high-pectin fruits should be used; be sure to test the juice before boiling. One important rule for a clear jelly, never squeeze juice from the cooked fruit.

TESTING PECTIN CONTENT

The natural pectin content of fruit varies with its ripeness – ripe fruit has less pectin – and the type of fruit. For instance, tart apples and plums are high in pectin, most ripe berries contain a medium amount, and apricots, peaches, figs and pineapple are low. Pectin can be judged from the fruit juice or pulp after it is cooked and before sugar is added. Mix 1 tablespoon of cooked fruit juice with 1 tablespoon of 70 per cent rubbing alcohol; fruit rich in pectin forms a large clot, a medium amount of pectin forms a few small clots, and fruit low in pectin deposits a bit of flaky sediment. If need be, liquid or powdered pectin can be added to fruit, but don't overdo it or the jelly or jam will be glutinous.

PACKING PRESERVES

This is just one of the various methods. I find small (250 ml/8 fl oz) jars with screw-top lids most practical as the contents are eaten quickly so don't spoil.

To sterilize, bring a large pan of water to the boil. Add jars and lids and boil 10 minutes. Remove and let dry on clean paper towels – don't wipe dry. Arrange jars on wooden board. Ladle preserves into jars while still very hot, using a funnel for jellies and thin jams, pouring others from a heatproof measuring cup. Fill to within 1 cm/⅜ inch of rim and, while still hot, cover with lid, fastening tightly. Cover with a cloth in case of leakage and turn jars upside down so preserves are in contact with lid; leave to cool. When cold, turn jars upright.

STAGES IN COOKING

▶ **UNDERCOOKED AND CLOUDY** – jelly too thin to hold a shape on a chilled plate; jelly thin and opaque, not translucent.

◀ **PERFECT** – on chilled plate, in 3-5 seconds a few drops set when pushed; sugar thermometer shows 106°C/220°F; bubbles break more slowly, not frothing.

▶ **OVERCOOKED** – jelly dark, sticky and too thick to spread; if very overcooked, flavour caramelized.

Fruit chutneys, confits & cooked relishes

Chutneys, confits and relishes are much less tricky than jams and jellies, thanks to spices and the acid in vinegar, which act as preservatives as well as flavourings. Far more than in other preserves, fruit and vegetables play a secondary role to seasonings and they must hold up well to the long cooking needed for flavours to mellow. In chutneys and confits, sugar is also a factor, toasting to a rich dark caramel — towards the end of cooking scorching is a danger, so watch out!

STAGES IN COOKING

▼ **UNDERCOOKED** – thin, often watery, lacking body; some ingredients still crisp; flavours not yet thoroughly blended; colours relatively pale.

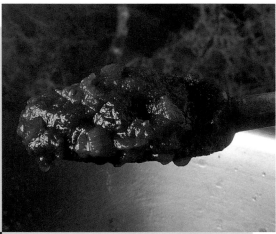

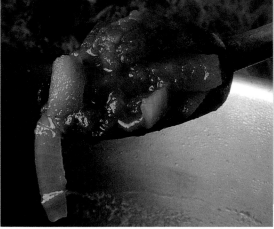

▲ **PERFECT** – thick enough to hold mark of spoon but still soft enough to fall from the spoon; all ingredients soft (for chutney and confit) or tender (for relishes); colour deep and rich; flavour intense with good balance of acid, sweet and savoury.

Apple and tomato chutney

Here's a great way to use the abundance of two autumn fruits!

MAKES ABOUT 3 LITRES/4²/₃ PINTS

1.8 kg/4 pounds ripe tomatoes

750 g/1¹/₂ pounds onions, sliced

400 g/13 oz dark brown sugar

1.25 litres/2 pints white wine vinegar

1 tablespoon ground ginger

2 tablespoons salt

2 teaspoons peppercorns

1.8 kg/4 pounds tart apples

Bring a large saucepan of water to the boil. Core the tomatoes and score an 'x' on each base. To peel them, immerse them in boiling water until the skin starts to split, 8-15 seconds. Transfer to a bowl of cold water. When cool enough to handle, peel the tomatoes and cut them into thick slices.

In a large bowl, combine the tomatoes, onions, sugar, vinegar, ginger and salt. Tie the peppercorns in a cheesecloth bag and add to tomato mixture. Cover and leave to macerate overnight in a cool place.

Peel, core and slice apples. In a large pan, combine the apples with the tomato mixture. Heat gently, stirring occasionally, until the sugar is dissolved. Bring the chutney to the boil and simmer until done, stirring often, about 1¹/₂ -1³/₄ hours.

Let the chutney cool for 4-5 minutes, then discard the peppercorn bag. Ladle the chutney into a heatproof measuring cup, pour it into sterilized jars and seal (see page 153).

Desserts

How conservative we are in our eating habits! A chef once told me that his dessert menu was almost impossible to change as customers clamoured for the same old favourites year after year. Certainly this collection bears him out. In this entire chapter only half a dozen dessert flavourings dominate – vanilla, chocolate, coffee, caramel, citrus and red berries. The ingredients are scarcely more varied, as most desserts rely on eggs, sugar, milk or cream, and possibly flour or a grain. Yet with this narrow palette we create a huge variety of firm favourites. We beat eggs for hot and cold soufflés and meringue, we set them in baked custards and use them to enrich many traditional hot puddings. We cook sugar to caramel or toast it with nuts to a praline, while chocolate is the common foundation of a dozen rich confections. Gelatine helps to set a series of cold desserts, and ice cream, sorbet and parfait form their own little group.

A dessert can be as simple as the crispy brown top of a baked pudding or as fanciful as the fluffy tower of a moulded cold soufflé. However, each one must make an impact, signalling the end of the meal – its last hurrah. Flavours must be vivid and colours dramatic, with the white of whipped cream and meringue, the gold of caramel and the darkness of chocolate. Think of the stained-glass-window colours of a molded jelly set with fruit, or the instant appeal of sorbet scooped into a frosted glass, or arranged in careful ovals on a plate.

So traditional are all these desserts that a quick glimpse tells you what is to come. Where does innovation enter? It appears in new flavours such as cape gooseberry, rose hip, or macadamia oil, and new combinations such as bread pudding made with panettone or a custard flavoured with lime. It comes with unexpected decorations such as a pointed spike of chocolate, or a sprig of basil instead of mint. The old custom of flaming a festive dessert is reappearing – why not? Here's where experimenting is up to you.

PANETTONE BREAD PUDDING, PAGE 163

DESSERTS

Whipping cream

When whipping cream, the important point to remember is that it turns to butter if you go too far. I learned this the hard way. When overwhipped, the butterfat in cream starts to separate and curdle. This happens more easily and rapidly if the cream is warm, so be sure to chill it, together with the bowl and whisk. To stiffen satisfactorily, cream must contain enough butterfat – 30 per cent is a minimum, and 40 per cent ('whipping cream' is about 35 per cent and double cream about 45) is better. Very high butterfat cream, over 50 per cent, can be heavy when whipped, so thin it with a little cold water. Sterilized cream, which contains stabilizer, stiffens more reliably than pasteurized cream but has much less taste.

When whipping cream, you'll find two distinct consistencies useful. At the first stage, the cream holds a fluffy, soft peak, just right for folding into other mixtures such as meringue or pastry cream. Continue whipping and the cream will become stiff enough to hold the firm peak needed for piped decorations. Take care, as if the cream is very stiff it may curdle slightly when forced through a star tube – we've all seen ragged rosettes of cream weeping at the edges. At any stage of whipping, a yellowish tinge signals that butterfat is coagulating and the cream is about to curdle; stop at once and chill the cream again before use. On standing, even stiffly whipped cream may separate slightly – simply beat it to recombine. Most commercial cream is bland stuff, I think, so unless it is to be mixed with other ingredients, after whipping I usually flavour it as Chantilly cream, with vanilla or Cognac and sweeten with caster or icing sugar.

STAGES IN WHIPPING

▶ **PERFECT FOR PIPING** – cream is fluffy and holds a stiff, well-defined peak when whisk is lifted; colour slightly deeper cream.

▼ **CURDLED** – cream wet and granular; colour yellowish from butter curds.

◀ **PERFECT FOR FOLDING** – cream is light and just holds a soft peak when whisk is lifted; colour pale cream.

Beating egg whites

For success, nothing is more important than correct beating of the egg whites to a fine, even texture incorporating the maximum of air. Constant beating with a balloon whisk is needed, gradually increasing speed to maximum as the whites froth and break up. Do not stop whisking before the whites are stiff. The whites themselves should be at room temperature, with no trace of moisture or fat, particularly any trace of egg yolk. (Fish out any egg yolk with nature's tool, the egg shell.) For once, very fresh eggs are not an advantage as they contain more moisture.

The type of mixing bowl also has an influence – the efficiency of copper is not just an illusion. A copper surface stabilizes egg whites so they can be beaten more easily to a smooth, close texture which holds well when folded with other ingredients. A copper bowl must be cleaned before use by rubbing it with 1 or 2 tablespoons salt and 1 or 2 tablespoons vinegar or a cut lemon. Rinse the bowl with water, dry it thoroughly and use within 15 minutes.

Overbeating is the greatest danger when whipping egg whites, particularly in a machine – they seem to coagulate suddenly and the texture coarsens, making them hard to fold smoothly into other ingredients. For savoury recipes, a pinch of cream of tartar slows stiffening and lessens the danger of overbeating. For sweet recipes, a tablespoon of sugar per egg white, whipped in when the whites are already stiff, acts as a stabilizer. If beaten egg whites do separate, they can usually be reconstituted by adding another unbeaten egg white for every 2 whites and whisking very vigorously until smooth again.

STAGES IN BEATING

▼ **TOO SOFT** – peak long when whisk lifted; whites floppy.

▼ **SEPARATED** – texture of whites granular, particularly at edges; whites pull away from sides of bowl and no longer hold clear, stiff peak.

▲ **PERFECT** – stiff enough to hold crisp peak when whisk is lifted; whites very smooth, appearance matt and clinging to sides of bowl with no trace of granular 'curdling'; bowl can be turned upside down without whites spilling.

Meringue

There are three types of meringue – simple, Italian and cooked – all of which are made with egg whites beaten with sugar. For a simple meringue, the only one made without heating the ingredients, the sugar is added to the beaten egg whites in two parts: first by beating thoroughly to dissolve the sugar and stabilize the whites, then by mixing more gently. This last stage used to be my downfall until I learned to stir until the meringue formed a long shiny peak, almost a ribbon. It should still, however, be stiff enough to pipe. Under- or overmixed meringue invariably weeps during baking, sticking, scorching and creating general havoc for the harried cook. Once mixed, simple meringue should be cooked very slowly so it dries rather than bakes – traditional cooks like to leave it in a low oven overnight. One hazard when working with meringue is humidity – a steamy kitchen or a damp day can seriously affect texture. Since meringue has a tendency to stick when baking, I suggest you use non-stick silicone paper or baking sheets.

Both Italian and cooked meringue bake and dry easily, to be smooth and dense but crisp. You'll find some recipes specify a relatively high temperature, so the meringue dries on the outside while the centre remains soft. Italian meringue, sometimes used as cake frosting and as a sweetener for whipped cream and parfaits, is made by whisking hot sugar syrup, cooked to the hard-ball stage (120°C/248°F), into beaten egg whites. For cooked meringue, egg whites and sugar are beaten together in a bowl over hot water until they froth and finally thicken to a firm white meringue.

STAGES IN BEATING

▼ **PERFECTLY BEATEN SIMPLE MERINGUE** – meringue mixture stiff and glossy; holds a long trailing peak when whisk is lifted; no trace of separation at edges.

▲ **PERFECTLY BEATEN ITALIAN MERINGUE** – very stiff and glossy with an almost glassy sheen; consistency tight, holding a sharp, very stiff peak.

Baked custards

It's amazing how many versions of baked custard can be created by adding a flavouring to three simple ingredients – eggs, milk and sugar. When whole eggs have been used for thickening, a custard can be unmoulded – 1 egg and 1 yolk per 250 ml/8 fl oz of milk is the usual proportion. Richer, softer custards such as pots de crème and crème brûlée are thickened only with yolks and cannot be turned out. Some custards are stabilized with cornflour or potato flour, but be sparing to avoid a taste of uncooked starch. Given its ingredients, a custard can be bland, so taste and adjust the flavour before baking. If you line the mould with caramel or a spoonful or two of tart jam such as redcurrant, it will dissolve and form a pleasant light sauce when unmoulded. Even simpler is a sprinkling of freshly grated nutmeg before the custard is baked.

All these custards are baked the same way, in a water bath so they cook gently and thoroughly in controlled heat. The water should come more than halfway up the side of the mould and I recommend lining the bath with a dish towel to discourage water bubbling into the custard. For more accurate timing, place the moulds in the bath and first bring the water to the boil on top of the stove. With the help of these tests you'll soon learn to recognize when a custard is done; remember it will continue to cook for a few minutes in its own heat – if overcooked, the custard will curdle to a coarse, bubbling texture for which there is no cure. Don't panic. Dare I say I quite enjoy the slightly chewy texture of an overbaked, curdled custard and I'm sure I'm not alone. Baked custards stiffen slightly as they cool and are normally served chilled.

STAGES IN COOKING

▼ SOFT AND THIN – skewer or tip of knife inserted in custard is moist, not clean; when mould is shaken, centre of custard is fluid and trembling.

▼ CURDLED – custard firm and skewer or tip of knife inserted in centre comes out clean; however, edges scorched; surface pockmarked with bubbles; texture coarse and full of bubbles.

▲ PERFECT – skewer or tip of knife inserted in custard comes out clean; when mould is shaken, centre of custard lightly set; texture very smooth and creamy; colour pale or deep yellow depending on egg yolks.

Batter puddings

Batter puddings, based on eggs, milk and flour, are a happy source of traditional desserts. Eggs lend lightness and the puddings may also be raised with baking powder. Many batter puddings feature fruits such as rhubarb, blackberries and fresh plums or prunes; the fruit should be quite tightly packed as the batter will flow easily around it. So the pudding rises well, with plenty of brown crust, I like to bake it in a shallow dish in a layer not more than 5 cm/ 2 inches thick. A dusting of sugar in the dish will caramelize nicely. I prefer the French gratin dishes of heavy cast iron for batter puddings, but heatproof glass or ceramic is good too. As for the batter itself, whole eggs and milk are the classic mix, thickened with a little (but not too much) flour. Cream in the batter is not an advantage as it can make the pudding heavy, but by all means serve plain cream, whipped cream or crème fraîche as an accompaniment. Savoury batter puddings such as popovers and Yorkshire pudding are part of the same family as dessert puddings. All are best served while still warm and puffy.

STAGES IN COOKING

▼ **UNDERCOOKED AND HEAVY** — flat and pale; flavour doughy.

▲ **PERFECT** — puffy, crisp edges with softer centre; top and bottom golden with browned edges, often glazed with caramelized sugar; flavour hearty.

Bread puddings

In a well-run kitchen, stale bread does not go to waste – hence the dozens of versions of bread pudding, most based on a sweetened custard of eggs and milk. A pudding is only as good as the bread you use to make it. Firm-textured breads are best, preferably a day or two old, so if the bread is moist, let it dry out in a low oven. Some cooks like to bake bread pudding in a water bath, but I find the brown crust – which is one of its attributes – to be less crisp. You can enrich bread pudding with ground almonds or coconut, or you can butter the bread, or layer the bread with dried fruits (don't sprinkle them on top as they will scorch). Many recipes add a wine such as port or Marsala. That's basically it – a quick family dessert which has recently hit the bistro circuit. A soggy or bland bread pudding can be much improved by sprinkling the surface of the pudding with sugar and grilling until caramelized.

STAGES IN COOKING

▼ **PERFECT** – pudding lightly set, golden brown especially around edges of bread; holds shape of spoon, but is not heavy; flavour mellow, lightly perfumed; colour creamy not grey.

▲ OVERCOOKED – texture dry and chewy; top often very brown and dry.

Panettone bread pudding

I first had this at one of London's finest Italian restaurants. When I tried it myself, I added some grappa, a pungent eau-de-vie – Cognac is an alternative. Serve the pudding with chilled double cream if you like.

SERVES 6–8

500 g/1 pound panettone
45-60g/1½-2oz butter
500 ml/16 fl oz double cream
125 ml/4 fl oz milk

75 ml/2½ fl oz grappa
4 eggs, lightly beaten
2 tablespoons sugar
pinch of salt

2-litre/3¼ pint soufflé dish

Preheat the oven to 160°C/325°F/gas3. Generously butter the soufflé dish. Cut the panettone into quarters lengthwise, then cut each quarter across in 2.5-cm/1-inch fan-shaped slices. Butter one side of each slice. Line bottom and sides of the soufflé dish with the panettone, buttered side inwards. Arrange the remaining slices in layers in the centre of the dish.

In a medium bowl, whisk the cream, milk, grappa, eggs, sugar and salt until foamy. Pour this mixture over the panettone. Press the slices down so they are submerged and let stand for 10 minutes so the bread soaks up the liquid. Cover the dish loosely with foil and bake in the preheated oven for 30 minutes. Uncover and continue baking until done, 30-40 minutes more. Serve warm.

Rice & grain puddings

Rice and grain puddings can be simmered on the hob, or baked very slowly in the oven. They will absorb four or five times their own volume of liquid (usually milk) while still remaining whole and plump. The amount of liquid absorbed depends very much on the type of grain. Round-grain rice, for instance, absorbs more liquid than long-grain varieties, at the same time yielding starch which thickens the cooking liquid to a rich cream. Sugar is normally added only near the end of cooking as it scorches easily. Grain puddings need more stirring on the hob than in the oven so, to avoid extra work, I usually bake rather than simmer them. If left uncovered in the oven without stirring at all, puddings with milk bake to an attractive brown crust. The same principle of simmering or baking in the oven holds good for puddings made with cracked or rolled grains such as oatmeal. Remember, a grain pudding will thicken considerably as it stands and cools.

STAGES IN COOKING

▼ **UNDERCOOKED AND THIN** — pudding watery, lacking richness; often grain is still chewy; flavour not yet developed.

▼ **OVERCOOKED AND HEAVY** — pudding is sticky, scarcely falling from spoon; rice grains have burst and fallen apart; if baked, pudding looks shrivelled; when tasted, pudding is pasty, flavour faded.

▲ **PERFECT** — liquid absorbed and grain creamy, falling easily from the spoon in a lightly thickened sauce; if baked, top forms a deep golden skin; when tasted, grains are very soft; flavour full-bodied and fragrant.

Steamed puddings

Anyone brought up in Britain, as I was, has surely enjoyed a moist steamed pudding redolent with spices and topped with golden syrup or honey. Variants often feature chocolate and dried and candied fruits. Batter for steamed puddings ranges from pound cake to gingerbread and age-old mixtures based on breadcrumbs and suet. During steaming, the pudding must be covered with paper and a cloth so humidity does not dilute the batter. For serving, be sure to include a topping of honey, golden syrup, custard, chocolate sauce or brandy butter. Steamed puddings reheat well and the most famous of all, Christmas pudding, is cooked twice: the first time so its dried fruits and nuts can be left to mature, the second time to reheat it before it goes, flaming in triumph, to the table. If you're unlucky enough to finish up with a pudding that's overcooked and dry, moisten it with orange or apple juice, piercing the pudding with a skewer so the juice penetrates.

▲ **PERFECT** – centre firm when pressed with a fingertip, and a skewer inserted into the centre of the pudding comes out clean; pudding well risen in mould; when the pudding is cut, the interior texture is even and light; the flavour is warm.

Dessert fritters

When you think about it, all sorts of doughs and batters can be fried as dessert fritters, from bread dough (doughnuts) to choux pastry (beignets), puff pastry (German Strauben) and sweet pie or biscuit dough (crullers, French bugnes, Spanish churros). Favourite street snacks with a quick coffee, fritters also form dessert when served with a honey or fruit sauce. As with all deep-frying, the temperature of the oil is key – for doughnuts and large fritters it should be 180°C/360°F, and higher at 190°C/375°F for smaller, thinner fritters like crullers. Flat fritters can also be fried in shallow oil, occasionally in butter.

The lightest fritters usually contain eggs or a raising agent, such as yeast or baking powder. Watch out for sugar, as doughs with a high sugar content brown quickly and scorch in hot oil. Deep-frying tends to overwhelm flavourings, though anise, cardamom and grated citrus zest hold up quite well. More commonly, sugar or honey and spices such as cinnamon are sprinkled on the fritters just before serving. Serve them quickly – light ones such as beignets hold up only a few minutes and even a doughnut is better when warm from the pan. Remember that if your fritters taste a bit oily, a squeeze of lemon juice will work wonders.

STAGES IN COOKING

▶ **PALE AND SOFT** – fritters (here choux pastry beignets) are puffed, but when cut open they are heavy and soggy with fat; browning is light or uneven.

◀ **PERFECT CENTRE** – brown and crisp on the outside, the fritters are hollow to the centre when split. Fritters are of even size, puffed and golden brown; all types of fritter are light and crisp, not fatty.

▶ **POORLY PUFFED** – fritters are small, heavy in the hand and often dark brown; centre is filled with uncooked dough.

Caramel

Caramel is simply toasted sugar – the tricky part is toasting it just right. For some purposes caramel should be light – for coating fruits for instance, or shaping those intriguing latticed cages to cover a dessert plate (the melted caramel is trailed over an oiled ladle, left to cool and set, then detached in one piece). When caramel is used as flavouring for a sauce or to line moulds for crème caramel, it should be darker. Just how dark is a matter of taste – I like caramel well done, almost piquant, but I don't have a sweet tooth. Many people like it paler, the colour of golden honey.

Caramel is usually made by boiling sugar syrup, though it is also possible to melt and then cook dry caster sugar. When boiling syrup, the danger is crystallization. Be sure the sugar dissolves completely before the syrup reaches the boil; do not stir during boiling and don't let any crystals dry on the side of the pan and fall back into the syrup. A spoonful of glucose or honey, a squeeze of lemon juice or a pinch of cream of tartar will deter the formation of crystals.

Cook at a steady rolling boil – take great care as the sugar's temperature rises to 165-175°C/330-350°F when it caramelizes and it can cause serious burns. As the water evaporates, bubbles will break more slowly until the syrup starts to colour. Then it caramelizes rapidly, so turn the heat down a bit. Swirl the pan occasionally, so the syrup colours evenly, and take it from the heat shortly before it reaches the right shade. Caramel burns quickly and irremediably and will keep cooking in the heat of the pan. To stop it cooking, at once plunge the base of the pan in cold water, or if making a sauce add the liquid.

STAGES IN COOKING

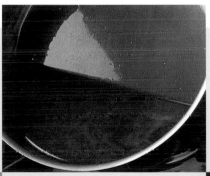

▼ **PERFECT LIGHT** — syrup well-coloured, showing pale golden when base of pan is tilted; sugar thermometer registers about 160°C/320°F.

▲ **PERFECT DARK** – syrup dark, showing chestnut brown on base of pan; starting to smoke; sugar thermometer registers 165-175°C/330-350°F.

▼ **BURNED** – syrup black, with thick, acrid smoke.

Ganache

Ganache is made by melting chopped chocolate with cream, either by pouring boiling cream over the chocolate, or by heating chopped chocolate with the cream. It's as simple as that. Flavour depends on the quality of the chocolate you use and I'd strongly recommend investing in the very best dark chocolate – the cost is justifiable as ganache is so rich you'll be using it in small quantities. The consistency of ganache depends on the proportions of cream to chocolate – for truffles and other firm confectionery, allow 125 ml/4 fl oz double cream per 250 g/½ pound of chocolate. More is needed for a ganache which is soft enough to spread as filling or frosting. One word of caution: with too little cream (less than 1½ teaspoons per 30 g/1 ounce of chocolate), ganache can seize and suddenly stiffen (see Melting Chocolate, page 137).

STAGES IN PREPARATION

▶ **PERFECT FOR SHAPING** – dark, pliable and stiff enough to hold a moulded shape; flavour dense.

▼ **LUMPY** – when cool, ganache is still liquid, with lumps at bottom.

◀ **PERFECT FOR FROSTING AND PIPING** – glossy and very smooth; stiff enough to hold a firm shape when piped, but still easy to spread; flavour mellow and rich; colour varies with type of chocolate.

Chocolate mousse

One of the first desserts I ever made as a child was chocolate mousse. It had two ingredients, melted chocolate and beaten egg whites – even without any flavouring it tasted pretty good. That's the joy of chocolate mousse and other fluffy chocolate desserts lightened with egg white – no matter what you do to them they remain edible, often delicious. You can angle them towards your audience, using milk chocolate for children or almond chocolate for lovers of nuts. My adult taste now inclines to dark chocolate enriched with cream and sharpened with rum or coffee. As well as a dessert, chocolate mousse is a lighter alternative to ganache as a filling for cakes and layered desserts, for instance of meringue. (See page 171 for mousses set with gelatine.)

STAGES IN PREPARATION

▼ **PERFECT** – texture smooth, fluffy and rich, set but not sticky; colour a glossy brown; flavour mellow.

▲ **SEPARATED** – texture granular and solid, speckled with egg white; on standing, liquid may separate to bottom of mousse; colour lacks gloss.

DESSERTS

Chocolate terrines

By definition, a chocolate terrine is firm enough to slice; by common accord it is also the richest, densest, lushest dessert you will ever encounter. Most often a terrine is based on dark chocolate, but layers of milk or white chocolate may be added. The mixture is set with butter or eggs, and nuts may be included, particularly chestnut purée. Mixing poses few problems, provided you respect the rules for melting chocolate (page 137). While I think of chocolate mousse as a family dessert, a chocolate terrine invites opulent decorations, such as chocolate curls, chocolate leaves, a spray of sugared redcurrants, a fan of pear poached in wine – possibly all at once. To contrast the richness, a sauce is mandatory, whether a pistachio or mint custard, or perhaps an orange and Grand Marnier cream.

STAGES IN **PREPARATION**

▼ **PERFECT** – smooth, rich texture, melting in the mouth rather than heavy; dense enough to slice; colour varies with chocolate used; taste of chocolate intense with undertones of flavouring such as liqueur or citrus zest.

▲ GRANULAR – texture coarse, slightly gritty; terrine may be heavy and solid, or moist and scarcely holding shape if eggs used; colour matt; flavour cloying.

Cold soufflés & mousses

Cold soufflés and mousses based on beaten eggs and set with gelatine are the stars of the buffet table. A ring of creamy mousse filled with macerated fruit, a fluffy soufflé towering high above its mould and crowned with chocolate leaves, a fruit charlotte walled with sponge cake, all are guaranteed to catch the eye. To please the palate as well, these delicate desserts need bold flavourings such as caramel, tart fruits like citrus, or liqueurs such as anise and pear. If a vivid ingredient such as raspberry or blood orange is available, so much the better, as soufflés and mousses are always lightened with whipped cream or beaten egg whites and can lack colour. Decorations of whipped cream, fresh or candied fruits, herb sprigs and curls of chocolate are de rigueur, plus a contrasting sauce.

When making cold mousses and soufflés, you need to be organized. Prepare the mould, measure the ingredients, whip the cream and soften the gelatine before you start beating the eggs. Assembly moves quickly and is dictated by the setting of gelatine. Whipped cream and beaten egg whites, folded in last of all when the basic mixture is about to set, must be at hand as most problems are caused by the mixture setting before all additions have been made. If the mixture doesn't fill the designated mould, this is a sign it is heavy and close-textured; be prepared to add height with a layer of berries, etc.! Of course, some mousses are not necessarily set with gelatine, especially if their principal ingredients have a solid enough consistency. The best example of this is, of course, Chocolate Mousse (see page 169).

STAGES IN PREPARATION

▼ **PERFECT** – soufflés (here, cold lemon soufflé) are very light and airy, just holding a shape; mousses are fluffy, just firm enough to unmould; flavour is delicate but lively; colour a clear pastel.

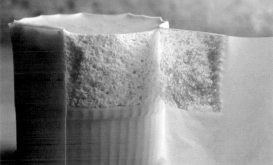

▲ **COARSE-TEXTURED** – mixture lumpy and dense, often showing strings of gelatine when spooned; texture is coarse on the tongue.

Ice creams

Nowadays, machines make home-made ice cream easy. I find ice cream mixtures more flexible than sorbet, less likely to form ice crystals from inadequate churning or too many watery ingredients. All that's needed is a base of egg custard or a similar rich cream. Yogurt-based mixtures and ice milk are alternatives. The richer an ice cream is with sugar, the lower its freezing point and the longer it takes to freeze, so chill the mixture thoroughly before churning; alcohol also has the same effect. Very rich, double cream has been known to separate if overchurned so I usually add it halfway, when the ice cream is at the slushy stage. Rich ice cream should hold well for a couple of weeks in the freezer.

Parfait is indeed 'perfect' so far as I am concerned. A simple mixture of egg mousse and whipped cream, parfait can be frozen without any of the churning needed for ice cream and sorbet. Flavourings may be plain, like chocolate, macerated dried or candied fruits, or the classic coffee, or as fanciful as caramel pecan, dried cherry with orange, or spiced apple sauce. When the children were small, I would add crushed Smarties. If you have leftover egg whites, you can use them in a parfait by substituting Italian meringue (see page 160) for the egg yolk and sugar mixture.

Always remember to let ice cream and parfaits soften for an hour or two in the refrigerator before serving.

▼ **PERFECT** – smooth, creamy and rich, but not cloying; soft enough to scoop with a spoon yet firm enough to hold a definite shape; flavour lively; colour clean.

◀ **PERFECT** – just soft enough to scoop with spoon; light but not fluffy, and very rich; flavour concentrated.

▶ **TOO HARD** – too stiff to scoop with a spoon; texture buttery on the tongue; flavour often bland.

172

Sorbets

The first sorbet I ever tasted, a children's party treat, was a solid lump of iced fruit juice. Some poor mother had not realized that constant churning is vital to break up the crystals which form as water freezes. Constant churning apart, much depends on the composition of the mixture itself. Sugar adds smoothness, though it lowers the freezing point and makes a mixture more difficult to set. A little lightly whisked egg white lightens and also discourages ice crystals, but a mere teaspoon per 1 litre/1⅔ pints of mixture is enough – too much makes it pasty on the tongue. Before you freeze a mixture, taste and adjust the flavouring. If the sorbet is to cleanse the palate in the middle of the meal, it needs less sugar. In any case, the flavour of a sorbet should be assertive – citrus, and acid fruits such as raspberry or passion fruit are favourites. Don't be tempted, however, to add too much alcohol as it lowers the freezing point, making it all the more difficult for the mixture to stiffen. If in doubt, spoon a spirit or liqueur over a sorbet just before serving. You'll find that a sorbet's flavour mellows after a few hours in the freezer. If frozen more than 12 hours, however, the texture will harden and you'll need to let the sorbet soften in the refrigerator before serving.

STAGES IN PREPARATION

▼ **PERFECT** – (here, lemon tea sorbet) smooth and firm enough to hold a clear shape when scooped with a spoon; flavour intense and refreshing; colour clean.

▲ **GRAINY** – texture gritty with ice crystals; shape jagged when scooped with spoon; colour cloudy.

Index

Numbers in *italics* refer to illustrations

Acknowledgements

I would like to extend warmest thanks to Virginia Willis, who has been my right hand in bringing this material to fruition. My other leading associates in the kitchen, on the studio floor, and at the editorial desk, have been Chefs Alexandre Bird and Laurent Terrasson, together with Kevin Tyldesley, Val Cipollone and Marah Stets (among many other things, the 'hands' in our pictures). I have also had valuable help at different times from Ken Atkinson, Tim Furst, Lin Hansen, Amanda Hesser and Bongani Ngwane. That's only half the story. There is also the team from Quadrille Publishing in London. I would like to acknowledge all those named on page 4, and particularly my editor Lewis Esson, who from start to finish worked with us so long and hard on this complex project. We all owe much to photographer Peter Williams - it is his vision and understanding, together with that of art director Mary Evans, that make it all work.